PARTS WORK

Also by Charles Johnston:

The Creative Imperative: Human Growth and Planetary Evolution Necessary Wisdom: Meeting the Challenge of a New Cultural Maturity Pattern and Reality: A Brief Introduction to Creative Systems Theory

The Power of Diversity: An Introduction to the Creative Systems Personality Typology

An Evolutionary History of Music: Introducing Creative Systems Theory Through the Language of Sound (DVD)

Quick and Dirty Answers to the Biggest of Questions: Creative Systems Theory Explains What It Is All About (Really)

Cultural Maturity: A Guidebook for the Future

Hope and the Future: Confronting Today's Crisis of Purpose

On the Evolution of Intimacy: A Brief Exploration into the Past, Present, and Future of Gender and Love

Rethinking How We Think: Integrative Meta-Perspective and the Cognitive "Growing Up" on Which Our Future Depends

Creative Systems Theory: A Comprehensive Theory of Purpose, Change, and Interrelationship in Human Systems (with Particular Pertinence to Un- Understanding the Times We Live In and the Tasks Ahead for the Species)

Perspective and Guidance for a Time of Deep Discord: Why We See Such Extreme Social and Political Polarization—and What We Can Do About It

Insight: Creative Systems Theory's Radical New Picture of Human Possibility

Intelligence's Creative Multiplicity: And Its Critical Role in the Future of Understanding

The Creative Systems Personality Typology: Engaging the Generative Roots of Diversity

Transitional Absurdity: A Reason for Hope / A Reason to Fear—Looking Squarely at the Future in Confusing and Contradictory Times

Online:

Author/professional page: www.CharlesJohnstonMD.com
The Institute for Creative Development: www.CreativeSystems.org
The Creative Systems Personality Typology: www.CSPTHome.org
An Evolutionary History of Music: www.Evolmusic.org
Cultural Maturity: A Blog for the Future: www.CulturalMaturityBlog.net
Ask the Cultural Psychiatrist YouTube channel: youtube.com/@cjohnston

PARTS WORK

Culturally Mature Identity, Relationship, and Leadership: A Method

CHARLES M. JOHNSTON, MD

The Institute for Creative Development (ICD)

Press Seattle, Washington

Publisher's Cataloging-in-Publication
(Provided by Cassidy Cataloguing Services, Inc.).

Names: Johnston, Charles M., author.

Title: Parts work : culturally mature identity, relationship, and leadership : a method / Charles M. Johnston, MD.

Description: Seattle, Washington : The Institute for Creative Development (ICD) Press, [2023] | Includes bibliographical references and index.

Identifiers: ISBN: 978-1-7342431-8-5 (paperback) | 979-8-9867952-1-8 (ebook) | LCCN: 2022924015

Subjects: LCSH: Typology (Psychology) | Temperament | Personality | Self-consciousness (Awareness) | Cultural pluralism--Psychological aspects | Social Evolution

Classification: LCC: HM626 .J64 2023 | DDC: 303.4--dc23

The Institute for Creative Development (ICD) Press, Seattle Washington
Copyright © 2024 by Charles Johnston, MD. All rights reserved. No part of this book may be reproduced, except for review and brief excerpts with attribution, without the written permission of the publisher. Manufactured in the United States of America. For information address The Institute for Creative Development (ICD) Press, 4324 Meridian Ave. N., Seattle, WA 98013, or CJ@creativesystems.org.

Cover design by Wilson Piechazek
Author photo by Brad Kelvin
Library of Congress Control Number: 2022924015
ISBN: 978-1-7342431-8-5
First Printing 2024

CONTENTS

Preface: Characters in a Play   7

Chapter One: Setting the Stage—The Method and its Applications   11

Chapter Two: Parts Work and Identity   23

Chapter Three: Parts Work and Conflict   37

Chapter Four: Parts Work and Relationship   48

Chapter Five: Parts Work and Big-Picture Questions   58

Chapter Six: Further Reflections—Putting the Method in Context   70

Afterword   83

Appendix A: Creative Systems Theory and the Concept of Cultural Maturity—An Introduction   84

Appendix B: Creative Context and Intelligence's Multiplicity   114

Index   132

PREFACE

Characters in a Play

Much of my life's work has come back to the recognition that our times are demanding new human capacities and new ways of thinking. Creative Systems Theory, the overarching theory of purpose, change, and interrelationship that is central to my contribution, describes the need for a critical next chapter in the human story. It calls this essential "growing up" as a species, Cultural Maturity.[1]

We can approach understanding Cultural Maturity theoretically; but because making sense of it requires that we reexamine not just what we think, but how we think, this can prove trickier than we might assume. We do better if we come at the notion more directly, in a more hands-on fashion. My purpose with this book is to introduce the hands-on approach that I have found most powerful. I call it simply Parts Work. Parts Work engages the whole of our cognitive complexity like characters in a play. Cultural Maturity challenges us to understand who we are and the world around us in more complete, more systemic ways. Parts Work, when done well, leaves us with almost no option but to step into Cultural Maturity's more embracing world of experience.

We can use Parts Work to address questions from the most personal to the most societal and encompassing. When applied in psychotherapy, it provides a straightforward approach that helps people make major strides in both their

---

[1] Appendix A provides a brief introduction to the theory and concept of Cultural Maturity. For more detail, see my book *Creative Systems Theory: A Comprehensive Theory of Purpose, Change, and Interrelationship in Human Systems*, 2021, ICD Press.

personal awareness and their relationships. When used in the training of leaders, it offers a direct way to address the complexities of current social conditions and to think with the greater systemic sophistication that questions of all sorts increasingly require.

To appreciate Parts Work's accomplishments and methods, it helps to look at the concept of Cultural Maturity. We can approach our understanding of Cultural Maturity in different ways, each of which has things to teach us. Right off, we can think about Cultural Maturity developmentally. Creative Systems Theory delineates parallels between a wide range of human formative processes, from simple creative acts to individual human development, to the growth of a relationship, to the evolution of culture. It also describes how we see a similar kind of cognitive reordering in the mature stages of these processes, and with it a new kind of defining story, including culture as a creative process.

We can also think of Cultural Maturity in terms of new capacities, which its changes make possible. These capacities include the ability to assume new and greater responsibility, not just for our actions but also for the truths we apply. Cultural Maturity challenges us to leave behind the practice of making culture a mythic parent, able to supply us with once-and-for-all truths. New capacities also include greater comfort with uncertainty and complexity and the ability to better acknowledge the fact of real limits; as well as an ability to get beyond polarized, ideological assumptions and think in more encompassing, systemic ways. And they also offer that we appreciate context: that what makes something true depends on when and where one looks.

Of particular importance for understanding Parts Work's results is the recognition that Cultural Maturity comprises changes in not only what we think, but how we think, a product of a developmentally predicted cognitive reordering. Cultural Maturity's changes involve stepping back from the whole of our cognitive complexity while at once deeply engaging with that complexity.

The theory's term for the result—Integrative Meta-perspective—while a bit of a mouthful, also captures the result quite precisely. If you think of a box of crayons, Integrative Meta-perspective lets us step back and separate ourselves from the individual crayons while drawing on their rich multiplicity of hues. The "whole-box-of-crayons" systemic vantage that results makes possible more nuanced—and ultimately wise—ways of thinking and acting.

Parts Work engages us directly in the changes that produce Integrative Meta-perspective—and no knowledge of Cultural Maturity is required. It invites us to confront the very questions that define our personal and collective lives in the context of a particular structure for inquiry. The result is whole-box-of-crayons understanding applied to concerns of every sort. Needed new capacities follow naturally from the effort, as do more mature kinds of principles for making choices.

My purpose with this short book is to bring the process of Parts Work alive; but it can only be an introduction. Fully appreciating the nuances of Parts Work requires watching it performed—or, better yet, taking part oneself—and that would need to occur over a significant period of time. As a psychiatrist, when I work with individuals using Parts Work, it is usually in weekly sessions for at least a year.

But even the bare beginning presented in these pages should prove powerful. Parts Work introduces important new steps in the evolution of psychotherapy. And along with supporting culturally mature change, it provides a hands-on definition for culturally mature perspective and a simple way to make sense of its implications. When engaged with greater depth, it helps clarify the conceptual foundations of Creative Systems Theory as a whole and the new ways of understanding that today's challenges increasingly require.

I have found it remarkable through the years that such a simple method can have such profound results. My hope is that in reading the book you will come away with a similar respect and appreciation for the approach. My hope, too, is that the practical immersion that the book provides can deepen your appreciation for the changes that the concept of Cultural Maturity describes.

Chapter One introduces Parts Work's particulars and the rules it follows. The subsequent chapters provide examples of the method as applied to different kinds of questions and contexts, beginning with Chapter Two, which applies the approach to questions of individual identity. Chapter Three shows how the approach works in the context of polarization and conflict, and Chapter Four turns to thinking about relationships more systemically. Chapter Five uses Parts Work to provide insight into more overarching, truth-related concerns, while Chapter Six brings together insights from early chapters to further fill out the approach and expand on its role in teaching us about Cultural Maturity and all it asks of us.

Appendix A introduces Creative Systems Theory (CST) and the concept of Cultural Maturity. If you have a conceptual inclination, it is a good place to begin. Alternately, you can dive right in and return to CST later, to further fill out the significance of what Parts Work accomplishes. Similarly, Appendix B provides supplemental information about contextual relativity and its resolute influences on cognitive and behavioral outcomes.

CHAPTER ONE

Setting the Stage—
The Method and Its Applications

Parts Work represents our various cognitive aspects—the "crayons" in our internal creative "box"— as characters in a play. This way of engaging our cognitive multiplicity might at first seem only metaphorical, but it becomes concrete and specific when viewed from a culturally mature vantage. Parts Work teaches people to appreciate and effectively draw on the entirety of these various aspects/characters. If a person is ready, and Parts Work is done well, the inherent result is Integrative Meta-perspective—at the very least, at the level of personal maturity. If the person can handle the challenge, we also see the acquisition of culturally mature perspective and culturally mature leadership abilities.

Parts Work can begin either with choosing a specific question or concern to explore; or with merely talking about one's life in general terms. The person, sitting in what will eventually be his or her Whole-Person chair (personally mature perspective chair—or perhaps, eventually, culturally mature perspective chair), is then guided in placing various parts around the room—perhaps a curious part, an angry part, a reasonable part, an intellectual part, a sexual part, each in its own chair (Figure 1-1). Through engaging in conversation with the various parts, the person learns to consciously draw on and apply his or her larger, whole-box-of-crayons complexity.

CHAIRS REPRESENTING PARTS

CHAIR REPRESENTING
WHOLE-SYSTEM
PERSPECTIVE

Fig. 1-1: Parts Work

Three cardinal rules guide the Parts Work process, each tying directly to the transition of our cognitive mechanisms to Integrative Meta-perspective. The first rule is that the Whole-Person chair (or Whole-System perspective chair, for larger cultural issues) provides the leadership in a culturally mature reality. Only the Whole-Person chair interacts with the world; and, through interacting with each of the parts, it draws on their contributions (Figure 1-2). This rule makes Parts Work a hands-on exercise for practicing culturally mature leadership—both in oneself and in the world.

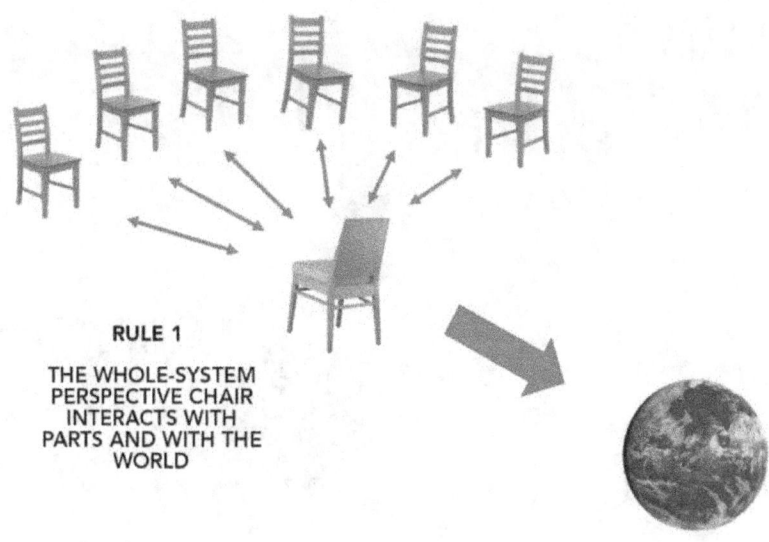

Fig. 1-2: Only the Whole-Person Chair Interacts with Parts and with the World.

The second rule follows from the first—Parts do not interact with the world (Figure 1-3). People doing Parts Work quickly recognize that engaging the world from parts, while it is what most people do most of the time, produces limited and limiting results. They also realize that their ideological beliefs—whether political, religious, or competing belief systems within their professions—can cause parts to take over and act as if they have a direct relationship with the world.

Fig.1-3: Parts Don't Talk to the World

The third cardinal rule is that parts do not talk to other parts (Figure 1-4). This recognition can take a bit longer to grasp, but it is ultimately just as critical. Much in the internal struggles of daily life is crosstalk between competing parts, and the implications are just as significant collectively. Parts talking to parts can cause us to confuse moderation or compromise with culturally mature perspective. In addition, less extreme ideological beliefs often have their roots in parts talking to each other. Creative Systems Theory explains the back and forth between competing worldviews over the course of history as a similar kind of conversation between systemic parts.

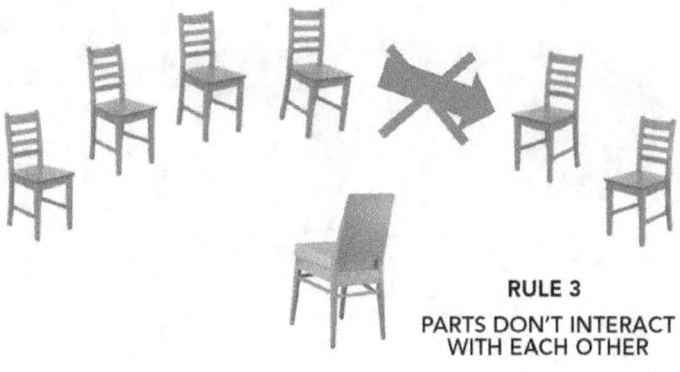

Fig. 1-4: Parts Don't Talk to Other Parts

Integrative Meta-perspective is an inherent result when we follow these cardinal rules. We can think of it as a kind of "cognitive rewiring." Wires are cut between parts and the world as well as between parts; while at the same time, people strengthen the wires that run between themselves and the world, and between themselves and their diverse and variously creative and contributing parts. Key to the power of the Parts Work approach is that the person does not need to know why it is working. Get the wiring right, and culturally mature understanding and culturally mature leadership capacities result naturally (Figure 1-5).

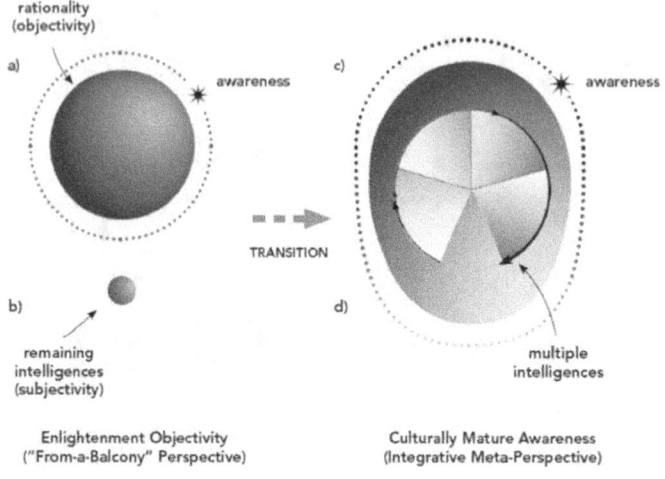

a) Rational intelligence (allied with awareness to produce from-a-balcony objectivity)
b) The subjective (all remaining intelligences as experienced in Modern Age reality)
c) < ------ * --------- > Culturally mature awareness in its various more and less conscious permutations[1]
d) Multiple intelligences (made newly explicit with culturally mature perspective)

Fig. 1-5: Cultural Maturity's Cognitive "Rewiring"

If Parts Work is being used to address an entrenched personal issue or a strongly held ideological belief, it may take a person some time to get to the place where these rules are honored; but the rules define the process. Importantly, they are also directly modeled in the room in the therapist's relationship with the client. For example, if a part attempts to talk to the therapist, the therapist directs its attention back to where it belongs, taking care to relate only to the person in the Whole-Person identity chair.

Parts Work effects multiple levels of experience. One possible result is finding new perspective for understanding the question at the work's starting point. But more important is how the method supports systemically holding experience as a whole. Through the dual process of simultaneously exercising authority from the Whole-Person chair while drawing deeply on the diverse viewpoints that the parts represent, the person becomes increasingly facile at engaging experience in more conscious and complete ways. At a personal level, the individual learns both to assume more conscious authority in their life and to draw more deeply on the diverse sensibilities that make them uniquely who they are. At a more cultural level, Parts Work engages the person in drawing consciously and deeply on the diverse sensibilities and inclinations that make us who we are as humans.

Parts Work and Psychotherapy

As a therapist, I use Parts Work to help people address internal conflicts and find more complete ways of being in the world. I consider the practice a major contribution—and a step forward—for psychotherapy. In actively drawing on intelligence's multiple aspects (unusual, though it is not alone in this regard), it places the final authority not with the therapist as interpreter, but in the hands of the person in the Whole-Person leadership chair—in contrast to most traditional methodologies. And while there are other approaches that work actively with parts (I think in particular of Fritz Perl's Gestalt therapy, Jacob Moreno's psychodrama, and Roberto Assagioli's psychosynthesis), the three cardinal rules mean that Parts Work as I have described it supports culturally mature growth in a way that other methods at best do indirectly. Of particular importance in this regard is that it is the person in the Whole-Person leadership chair (not the therapist/facilitator) who talks with parts, something not found in any other method that I am aware of.

Therapeutic work that occurs over time tends to proceed through recognizable stages, each stage being key to Integrative Meta-perspective's changes. The first stage involves learning the difference between coming from the perspective of the Whole-Person identity chair and coming from the perspective of a part. The emphasis with this first kind of process is on separation and distinction. It involves recognizing how identifying with parts inherently produces distorted beliefs and polarized relationships. And it involves learning to say "no" when parts attempt to take over.

With the next stage, the focus turns to the Whole-Person chair. I will often have the person make "leadership statements" to the parts, both to clarify who is in charge and to help the person become more adept at asking the kinds of questions that ultimately need to be asked in order to make culturally mature choices. I also encourage the person to identify challenging life situations where they can practice making decisions from the Whole-Person/Whole System chair's vantage.

The final stage involves a new and deeper kind of engagement with parts. Once people gain confidence in leading from the Whole-Person chair, they can turn their attention to drawing on different aspects as they can provide benefit. The results are frequently surprising. Often parts have contributions to make that the person had not anticipated. And the greatest surprise is frequently how richly potent and creative life can become when the person successfully draws on the full depth of their complexity.

As a therapist, over the years I've come to draw more and more on the Parts Work approach. In part this is because of the directness and simplicity of the method. But it is also because, whatever the issue the work may focus on, it helps prepare a person for the mature kinds of thinking and acting our world increasingly demands. I don't know of other techniques that apply all of intelligence's multiple aspects so simply and unobtrusively. Neither do I know of other ways of working that support the various aspects of culturally mature understanding, and not just through what is said, but through every aspect of the approach, including the layout of the room. Of particular significance is the fact that I as a therapist speak only to the Whole-Person chair (in keeping with the first cardinal rule), creating a relationship with the client that models and affirms relationship of a Whole-Person sort.

Parts Work is not a "quick fix," even if the focus is primarily on personal concerns. But over time, more encompassing ways of thinking and acting follow naturally from the process. Eventually Parts Work alters not only how a person addresses specific issues, but also how he or she engages reality more broadly. The work becomes like lifting weights, to build the "muscles" of culturally mature capacity. One of the litmus tests for success with this way of working is the appearance of culturally mature shifts regarding questions that had not been addressed.

Parts Work and Culturally Mature Leadership

In training leaders, I use Parts Work to address conflicting societal beliefs and to help people grasp how ideological conclusions that might seem incompatible reflect aspects of a needed larger systemic picture. In this way, people experience important recognitions central to culturally mature understanding by doing Parts Work.

For example, Parts Work provides confirmation of Creative Systems Theory's observation that ideological beliefs reflect identification with systemic aspects. In doing Parts Work, people find it increasingly obvious that parts by their nature hold simplistic and limited beliefs. People also see that allowing parts to talk to the world (in violation of the second cardinal rule) results in reactive and ideological assertions. In later chapters, we will see how the first-hand experience of culturally mature leadership provided by doing Parts Work confirms how such leadership is at once more powerful and humbler than that which it replaces.

I will also describe how this same general kind of approach can be applied when working with more than one person. When assisting groups where issues have become polarized, or organizations where people wish to address many-sided questions that require careful, in-depth inquiry, I often use related methods. When working in this way, I place individuals or small subgroups around the room to represent the various systemic aspects of the question at hand. Another group takes the Whole-Person chair role and attempts to articulate a larger systemic perspective. In my book *Perspective and Guidance for a Time of Deep Discord*[2], I apply Parts Work to an array of highly polarizing issues—climate change, health care reform, race and gender, abortion, immigration, and more.

Polarity, Fallacies, Capacitance, and Symptoms

In getting started, a few additional Creative Systems notions are important to note. While each in its own way helps guide us in using Parts Work and understanding its implications, they also play important roles in the examples I offer in later chapters.

A couple of Creative Systems Theory concepts are particularly helpful for understanding how a person might lose their way psychologically, and what happens when they do. One is the concept of Capacitance, which represents how much of life a system can tolerate. Next, the concept of Symptoms, as defined in the theory, refers to ways that systems may respond when stretched beyond their available Capacitance. Think of a balloon that if blown up too fully might break. It may continue to grow, or a system may respond in some way that limits the challenge to Capacitance—become aggressive, withdraw, become overly rational or overly emotional, manic or depressed, abusive or undermining, and so on. We can understand any of these responses in Parts Work terms. When Systems feel overwhelmed, they become vulnerable to parts taking over and inappropriately influencing one's response.

A further recognition—that parts tend to exist in polar relationships—helps with understanding why parts take the forms that they do. They tend to juxtapose qualities that are more archetypally masculine (harder, more

---

[2] *Perspectives and Guidance for a Time of Deep Discord*, ICD Press 2021.

concerned with difference) with qualities that are more archetypally feminine (softer, more concerned with relationship). We see this with polarities like thoughts versus feelings or expressive versus receptive. Most obviously, this observation clarifies why parts may act as they do, and explains the relationships they form with each other. But while identifying with parts necessarily leaves a person lacking culturally mature understanding, it also provides insight for understanding a person's or group's particular blindnesses.

Expanding on the concept of polarities, Creative Systems Theory identifies three kinds of polar fallacies: Separative Fallacies, Unity Fallacies, and Compromise Fallacies. Separation Fallacies occur when we take an archetypally masculine part and make it the whole of truth. Unity Fallacies result when we accept an archetypally feminine part as the whole truth. And Compromise Fallacies happen when we confuse finding compromise between polar parts with Whole-Person/Whole-Systems perspective. Parts Work helps clarify where a person may be falling into one of these conceptual traps and offers a concrete way to get beyond it and learn to think in larger ways.

Systemic Perspective's Larger Implications

Parts Work can also be used to engage overarching questions more systemically. For example, in my book *Creative Systems Theory*, I describe how it can help reconcile the most timeless and persistent of polarities—that which divides the material and the spiritual: science and religion. The way that Parts Work, when done well, equally challenges the assumptions of someone who identifies with either scientific or religious conclusions further highlights how culturally mature perspective is new in a fundamental sense and illustrates the power of Parts Work.

Someone of a scientific bent doing Parts Work is likely, at least initially, to assume that the part that thinks rationally and scientifically sits in the Whole-Person/Whole-System chair. Given that this is where the person has often most found significance, it is not an unreasonable assumption. But before long it becomes clear that this part is limited in what it has to contribute to many issues of no small importance in one's personal life, such as purpose or love. Eventually, the person comes to recognize that more than this part is needed not just for making good life choices, but for the most filled-out and creative kind of science.

Something very similar tends to happen for people with spiritual inclinations, whether they be traditional religious beliefs, humanistic "spiritual but not religious" tendencies, or of a New Age bent. Commonly the person will assume that spiritual truth appropriately sits in the Whole-Person/Whole-System chair. And again, for them, this is not an unreasonable conclusion. But if such a person works long enough, they recognize in a similar way that having spiritual truth sit in the Whole-Person/Whole-System chair in our time leads to problems. An all-too-common result is poorly-thought-out life choices and unsuccessful relationships. It turns out that, in a well-lived life—a spiritual life in the best sense—the manifest parts of existence are as important as the essences. Eventually, the person may realize that holding the spiritual more systemically in this way will lead not only to making good everyday choices, but to the most full and creative relationship to spiritual experience.

In doing Parts Work, the chairs that advocate for aspects of larger truths—whether personal truths or truths of a social or even philosophical sort—each in important ways add to the Whole-Person/Whole-System perspective chair's reflections. But they function, at best, as consultants. When we miss this fact, unhelpful, indeed dangerous ideological conclusions result. With Parts Work, people confront this recognition not just as some abstract conclusion, but immediately on a personal level. Living from the Whole-Person/Whole-System chair is the ultimate task with culturally mature leadership—whether in our personal lives or more broadly. We can think of doing so as what ultimately defines today's needed new common sense.

CHAPTER TWO

Parts Work and Identity

Let's start with some examples of Parts Work that engages personal concerns, what one might commonly find in psychotherapy. In each of these examples, Parts Work helps a person draw on the whole of who they are. It also helps the person be most effective regarding the things in life that matter most to that person. In these examples, Integrative Meta-perspective is engaged primarily at the level of personal maturity; but in each case, at least a foundation is set for a more culturally mature relationship with identity.

Parts Work highlights an essential new kind of responsibility when it comes to identity. I become responsible for doing everything I can to make my life choices from that Whole-Person chair. In a culturally mature reality, the Whole-Person chair has as much to do with the "growing up" of culture as with new maturity as an individual. It is a new reality that loops back on itself. When I fail at this larger responsibility, I also fail myself. When I accept it, my daily choices provide not just personal leadership, but also leadership in the world around me.

Dale—Anger and Procrastination

Dale was the forty-year-old head of a small, family-run construction company when he came to me seeking therapy. His father had just retired and handed the reins of the company over to him; but overseeing the business was proving more demanding than Dale had anticipated. When he felt overwhelmed, his temper could get the best of him, often enough that it was getting in the way of his being effective.

Therapy was obviously not a familiar environment for Dale. Stocky in build and generally affable in meetings, he was clearly not comfortable sitting with me in the room. But he knew that something needed to change: He didn't understand why he was reacting as he was and could see he was losing the respect of those working for him.

After a few sessions of getting acquainted, I briefly introduced Parts Work. The place to start was obvious: Dale had a defensive part that was easily triggered. I asked Dale to imagine that part sitting on a chair in front of him and to describe everything he could about it.

The part was young, a bit tense, and fidgety. I asked Dale how he felt as he looked at the part. At first Dale commented that he didn't really want to look at it; but eventually he observed that mostly he felt sad for the part. He felt like the part was a basically good kid, but he was clearly over his head when it came to being boss of a company. He saw that the part's anger was an effort to protect him, a way to keep the world at bay.

Dale then commented that he felt odd thinking of the part as separate, making him only a part. I responded that doing so was a powerful and necessary first step. It made it possible to get some distance from the feelings. It also affirmed that he in his chair could be in charge and perhaps provide some protection and perspective so the part could feel safer. We talked at some length about the importance of recognizing that the part was a only a part, not him. Before he left, I gave Dale the homework that, if at any time he began to experience those reactive feelings, he would step away from them and get back into his own chair.

In the following session, Dale reported that his homework task was easier said than done. But he also described how beginning to get this kind of separation had been helpful. After introducing the concept of leadership statements, I asked Dale to state, from his chair, why this kind of distinction was important and how he would be drawing on it in the future.

We also discussed ways in which he could better protect that reactive part. He saw that at times he tried to take on too much; and, in addition, that he could better prepare for situations where he would need to make decisions. Dale recognized that it was possible to plan for potentially overwhelming situations. I coached Dale to share these thoughts with the reactive part and ask if this would make it more comfortable. I then had Dale sit in the reactive part's chair and see how the part felt in response. It was clear that having Dale in charge and prepared with a plan made the reactive part more comfortable.

As Dale and I talked, I suggested one more change that might not make sense at first, but that would prove particularly important in the long run. The change dealt with the part's practice of scanning the world for dangers, and in so doing, taking over. I suggested that the part should have no relationship with the world, only with him. The part could watch him to be sure he was being adequately attentive to dangers; but it was Dale's job to be discerning about the world, not the part's. This practice was added to Dale's homework.

Soon thereafter, another important topic came up in our sessions. Dale realized he often put off things that needed attention. His procrastination was becoming a major problem as needed leadership tasks in the business piled up. In fact, the company risked collapse if he could not get more on top of things.

This seemed like a good segue for bringing more parts into the room. When I asked Dale who it was that dug in its heels, he responded that it felt like a slightly overweight guy in the opposite corner.

As Dale confronted this new part and asked what was going on, the part admitted involvement. It became clear that this part was also trying to protect Dale, in that procrastination shielded him from having to deal with things that might overwhelm him. Quickly seeing that this didn't really provide a solution, Dale realized that, in the long run, putting things off only increased his feelings of anxiety.

Dale tried some of the same strategies with this part. He tried talking to it, creating distance, and doing a better job of providing protection. But this time, it seemed to have much less of an effect. Whatever was going on was obviously more complex than just this part taking over. Further conversation with the part revealed that its resistance was not just protective; it was struggling against something. Clearly there were other parts involved in the dynamic.

It turned out to be his old friend, the angry/reactive part. Only this time, rather than acting out in the world, it was engaging in a more internal kind of combat: bullying the part that was procrastinating. Even more than protecting Dale from the world, the procrastinating part was protecting itself from the internal bully.

After taking some time to reflect on this, Dale shared a memory from early in life. As a child, he often compared himself to his brother who, besides being older, was also quicker on his feet and admittedly smarter than Dale. Growing up, Dale could feel like he didn't measure up; and the fact that his brother could at times be a bully didn't help.

I told Dale to bring this original, angry/reactive part, now in its manifestation as the demanding bully, into the room so that he could confront him. This part clearly thought it knew best; and in talking with Dale, it made clear that it didn't like or respect the other part.

I then introduced the concept of crosstalk. It was obvious that the demanding bully part was talking with the procrastinating part. And it was also obvious that the procrastination part, by digging in its heels, was effectively keeping the bullying part from taking over. It was not just protecting itself; it was also providing protection for Dale.

Dale and I talked about the rewiring that needed to be done. He needed to stop the crosstalk—to cut the wire between the two parts—and at the same time establish a strong connection between himself and each of the parts. He also needed to cut the wires between each of the parts and the world, not only to keep each part from taking over but from interacting with the world at all. Each was to engage only with Dale.

Over the weeks and months that followed, Dale practiced this new kind of cognitive mapping, making every effort to engage the world only from his chair and to notice when parts tried to take over. He got much better at noticing when crosstalk was taking place. At first the parts were not always happy with these changes, but as time went on it became increasingly obvious that things were getting better for everyone.

In the months that followed, Dale's conversations with these two parts revealed how much this was the case.. Obviously, the procrastinating part felt safer and less abused when protected from the crosstalk. But there was more. The deeper connections within Dale provided a new depth of insight into the things that were most important in his daily life. Dale saw that the angry/reactive part had been triggered in the past when things that mattered were threatened. Now that it felt safer, that part became less reactive, and more just a sensitive part. It could help Dale fine tune his understanding of the values and life directions that he finds most meaningful.

A similar kind of evolution took place through Dale's conversations with the angry/reactive part: Over time, he learned to prevent it from taking over in his role as boss in the workplace. And similarly, Dale got better at noticing when crosstalk was causing inner bullying. But that part could be an asset, Dale discovered, when he needed to take a strong stand. And he also saw that keeping up a dialog with that part could help him identify what was worth standing up for.

The results were new empowerment and creativity all the way around, certainly for Dale, now that he led more explicitly from his Whole-Person chair. But it was also the case that each part could now be better appreciated and more effectively used. This change made Dale a much more fulfilled and effective leader of his company and within himself.

Rebecca and the Making of Major Life Choices

The second example comes from a thirty-two-year-old first-grade teacher who needed to decide whether she wanted to continue teaching. This scenario is more complex than the last for its drawing on multiple parts and the added variable of personality style.

Rebecca had been teaching for eight years in a traditional public school in one of the city's poorer neighborhoods. Her students comprised a broad mix of ethnic backgrounds and countries of origin, with English often their second language. Creative and slightly quirky, Rebecca was sensitive to the needs of young children and diverse populations; but her makeup was fragile, making certain aspects of her job more challenging than they might have been for more conventional teachers. In particular, Rebecca's temperament made setting strict boundaries, a necessary ability for a teacher, very difficult, especially in complex environments. And, in general, she did not feel supported by the school, which relied on more traditional methods than those she preferred.

On first coming to see me, Rebecca reported being constantly anxious and sleeping poorly. Often self-critical and feeling inadequate as a teacher, she had pretty much decided that she was not cut out for teaching and was ready to quit. But in initially talking with Rebecca, it was clear to me that she was in fact an exceptional teacher. Highly sensitive and deeply appreciative of her students, she brought real creativity to the classroom. However, while she was highly gifted, her circumstances were making demands that were neither healthy nor sustainable.

After a few initial sessions with me, once Rebecca felt comfortable, I asked her to describe everything she could about the part of herself that was feeling anxious. The way I spoke at first took Rebecca aback. She had not thought of her anxiety as a "part." But she was willing to play along and soon brought the part into the room, placing it in the chair to her right. At the end of the session, Rebecca commented that, while working this way felt strange, addressing the anxious part directly did seem to help her feel more relaxed.

In the next session, as Rebecca more actively engaged the anxious part and responded from its chair, it described itself as feeling unsafe and said that it wanted to run away. It also said it was angry at Rebecca for not protecting it, a comment that surprised and confused Rebecca. To help her gain perspective, I asked if this part played any positive role in her teaching. She realized that it very much did: It was a sensitive part that she often drew on in relating to the kids. I then asked whether this part was often doing the relating. She realized that frequently it was.

Rebecca and I then discussed these revelations. I observed that the same tendencies that gave the anxious/sensitive part its sensitivity would prevent it from grasping the importance of boundaries, and that the only way it had to protect itself was to flee. Explaining that the problem was really more fundamental, I then described the three cardinal rules, emphasizing that it was only the Whole-Person chair's job to make the choices and do the relating—and how problems inevitably result when parts relate to the world. I also pointed out that a further essential part of the Whole-Person chair's task was to take charge in setting boundaries. We agreed to talk in later sessions about learning to set better boundaries as a teacher—and in her life as a whole.

The next session brought attention to another part, and also to an important additional boundary. The anxious part described feeling the presence of a rational part, which could appear critical. But when asked if the people around her were critical, Rebecca said they had in fact been quite supportive. Therefore the criticism was coming from a critical part within herself.

I suggested that Rebecca also bring this rational part into the room, and she placed it in the chair to her left. Again she described relief simply in giving the part a chair—in this case because it helped her appreciate that, rather than being an outside influence, it was something that she could possibly affect.

As she talked at length with the rational part, Rebecca was struck by the lack of maliciousness in its criticisms—how it really just wanted her to do well. But she saw, too, how its actions could produce harmful results. And as she worked, Rebecca recognized another important concern about the rational part: It was talking not just to her, but also to the anxious part. The rational part was breaking the cardinal rule that parts don't talk to parts; and, given that the anxious part had no way to protect itself, such "crosstalk" was going to be particularly problematical. Rebecca saw that leading from her Whole-Person chair would require her to set not just better boundaries in the world, but also better internal boundaries. She would need to stop the crosstalk, to be sure that the critical part communicated only with her.

I suggested an exercise that might help Rebecca practice these needed new leadership skills. I proposed specific classroom challenges and Rebecca responded with ways she might handle them differently. She discovered to her fascination that both her anxious/sensitive and rational/critical parts—once she had the right kind of relationships within them—could be of help. She saw that the sensitive part, formerly known mostly through feeling anxious, helped her to be empathetic toward students, to appreciate their different needs, and to sense when she was starting to feel overwhelmed. She saw also that the more rational part, which she had known mostly through unhelpful negativity, could help bring clarity to places where boundaries in the world were needed and help her find the courage to set them.

While the exercise in itself proved helpful, it also highlighted further work that would be essential. If Rebecca was to rethink how she taught, she would need to better understand what was important to her as a teacher—to understand her own values and explore the teaching approaches that would best serve them. Rebecca recognized that she would need to involve other aspects of herself in using Parts Work to provide assistance towards these goals. Over the ensuing weeks she brought in a playful/creative part, a strongly ethical part, a no-nonsense part, and a part that loved big-picture understanding. After many useful "ahas," Rebecca was able to describe the values and priorities that were most important to her.

Eventually we returned to the exercise of trying on classroom challenges. Rebecca would imagine scenarios and use her parts to brainstorm how she would manage them. This included working with students who had different kinds of needs and classroom situations that might involve conflict or scary interactions. Rebecca was pleased to see that, in most situations, if she kept her values in mind she knew what to do. She also recognized that in situations where she didn't immediately know, some conferring with her parts often not only revealed workable strategies, but also inspired her to try them in her classroom. In working with her parts, Rebecca was also encouraged by how much her sense of what mattered to her deepened. When she addressed questions from the whole of herself, she ended up thinking about learning and teaching—indeed, the whole purpose of education—in new, more creative ways. Although she found some of this daunting, she also felt the beginnings of a new excitement in the teaching process.

When I asked Rebecca if this new excitement was enough to have her consider teaching again, her recognition that she was still unsure alerted her to a further essential topic: To make her decision, she would need to reexamine her relationship with the school. Specifically, she recognized the importance of setting better boundaries there.

Some of these boundaries were simple and easily accomplished. For example, whereas she had always assumed she should share lunch each day with the other teachers in the teachers' lunchroom, she realized that sometimes it would be better to spend time alone to recharge herself. She also realized that faculty meetings often seemed to have little value and could leave her drained; so she decided she would find out from the principal when attendance was important and when it was optional. Finally, Rebecca realized something that at once excited and disturbed her: If she was going to stay on at the school, she would need to speak out in new ways. The school needed to make changes in order to be a quality learning environment, and Rebecca would need to advocate for those changes if she was going to remain happy there.

Some sessions later, I again asked Rebecca how she was feeling about being a teacher. She responded that while in many ways the thought seemed even more overwhelming, it was also seeming more interesting. On hearing this, I asked Rebecca a further question that we had not touched on, but that I suspected would provide insight into the choices she would need to make. I asked her whether working at a different school, one that was more innovative and perhaps with a less challenging student population, might be a better fit.

She decided to try this additional question out with her parts. Again she found surprises. Their responses helped her recognize that much of what made teaching fulfilling for her was the diverse and challenging population. The parts' responses also helped her see that if she assumed the kind of leadership in herself we had been working on, she would likely be strong enough to handle what would be required.

Rebecca did decide to stay on. It was nearing summer break and the time away would give her a chance to get ready for the new year. Over that year we continued to work together, and she continued to practice her new skills. Much did not become easier. Indeed, teaching and the school environment became even more demanding. But her effectiveness as a teacher grew and she found increasing fulfillment in her role as an educator.

Several years later we crossed paths again. I was just then starting an ongoing think tank on the future of education at the Institute I was directing. In time Rebecca would become a valued member.

Tim and Today's Crisis of Purpose

This chapter's third example comes from work with a twenty-year-old whom I will call Tim. While work with Tim was primarily personal, it also tied directly to a critical culture issue that Creative Systems Theory calls our modern Crisis of Purpose. At the time of this writing, the description ends more with a question than with resolution.

Although it was obvious to me that he was a bright person with a great deal of potential, on first meeting Tim I had major concerns about what might lie ahead for him. I mean this not just in the sense of whether his life would take a gratifying course, but simply whether he would survive into adulthood. Addictive behavior consumed a major portion of his time: many hours a day playing video games, dependence on alcohol and marijuana, and, off and on, the use of prescription painkillers. He was dangerously adrift.

In our early sessions, I asked simple questions about Tim's daily life and what was important to him. We talked generally about interests and strengths, and about values. While his life lacked direction, Tim was capable of being reflective, and he often voiced strong opinions. Thankfully his Whole-Person chair was at least sometimes available to engage. Because Tim had major questions about what he wanted to do with his life, he benefited from this basic work. But while these early sessions were useful and established trust, it was obvious that he was keeping the most important issues at arm's length. Finally, Tim announced, "We have to talk about the elephant in the room—how addicted I am to distraction."

Parts Work seemed like a natural match for Tim's needs. I briefly introduced what it involved and invited Tim to give the part that was addicted to distraction a chair. I told him to describe the part, observing everything he could about it. When he finished, I asked Tim how much of the time that part was in charge. He said probably 80 percent of his waking hours. This was a hard thing for him to admit.

Initially, Tim found it hard to distinguish himself from the part; simply creating needed separation took multiple sessions. But in the process of going back and forth between himself and the part's chair, gradually Tim made progress differentiating the two. He also began to realize how important learning to be in charge from his Whole-Person chair was going to be if his life was going to work.

That was a start, but the way Tim was thinking about addiction—simply that it was bad and that he has to do better—was not going to get him where he needed to go. I informed Tim that taking charge required something more powerful than the addictive part could provide.

Tim's conversations with the distracted part pointed to a path forward. When Tim asked the part why it took over, it answered that it felt hopeless—and not just about Tim's life. The part described how, when it looked at all that is going on in the world, it often felt hopeless about that as well. The part proposed that, given what it saw, distraction was the safest and most rational choice.

Although the part's answer startled Tim, he appreciated that the part was being honest—and not unreasonable. When asked if he, in his Whole-Person chair, also felt hopeless, Tim was not sure. If given the choice between distraction and looking squarely at the truth no matter how difficult, would he also choose distraction?

There was a long pause as Tim realized that his answer would determine not just the course of therapy, but also of his life. Finally he said he would choose the truth, even though it scared him to say so. From what I knew of Tim, I thought that was indeed the case, and told him so. I too had deep concerns about Tim's future.

This exchange brought us back to where our sessions had begun: finding a set of values and priorities more important to Tim than his addictions. And it was about Tim finding the courage to incorruptibly follow those values and priorities in shaping his life. We agreed that therapy going forward would be about looking unswervingly at the truth. With this agreement, our work began in earnest.

Tim observed that when it came to values, he often felt confused, pulled back and forth between opposing conclusions. Tim was not lacking in strength as a person. But he did very much lack a picture of his future that in any way stood up to scrutiny. In my opinion, identifying more parts would help shed light on these internal conflicts. It would also challenge Tim to get beyond them.

Tim had already recognized that the final answer did not lie in his distraction part's view of the world. So we tried adding new parts to see if they might offer better direction. The next part he added was a reflection of the models Tim had grown up with. Tim's parents had wanted him to go to business school or perhaps become a lawyer. In talking with that part, Tim realized that neither of these options were a good fit for him. While each reflected values he could respect, they didn't speak to what mattered most to him. He also saw that some of his vulnerability to distraction was a reaction to choices that did not give his life meaning.

Tim next turned to a part that spoke for a direction many of his peers were taking, including his best friend, who had become a software engineer. Tim liked that this direction had a promising future and would make use of his intellect. But in talking to the part, he quickly learned that this direction was not sufficiently compelling, either.

Tim's next thought was that he needed to do something with people, possibly in the social services, and identified a liberal part that advocated for the disadvantaged. But again, conversations with this part proved in the end no more fruitful. While he shared many values with this part, he could not help feeling that its ideas were naive. He concluded that following that part's advice would not lead to meaningful outcomes or a life that satisfied him.

At this point I confronted Tim. When people reject the advice of all their parts, very often they are in fact in a part themselves and are merely avoiding commitment. I wasn't sure this was the case for Tim; but if it was, I wanted him to acknowledge it.

When I described my concern and asked Tim what he thought, he responded that engaging these various parts had in fact made him more committed to making a contribution. He also observed that the parts he had identified had not been wholly unhelpful: Each had had something valuable to add to the conversation. He admired a rigor in the part that advocated for more traditional roles; the part that leaned toward a technology career brought a visionary quality he liked; the part that emphasized liberal values, while simplistic in its conclusions, was at least putting values forefront; and even the part that spoke for addiction had something to contribute. In contrasting himself with it, he was reminded of the importance of courage and commitment even in the face of what might seem discouraging realities.

Tim continued to explore values and priorities, considering directions consistent with them. In drawing on his various parts, his strength and confidence grew to the point where addiction stopped being a concern, since Tim was finding life too interesting and important. His next steps were not yet clear, but I had no question that Tim will make an important contribution in his life. With each session, he brought greater courage to looking at himself and the future. Tim did what our times are in some way asking of all of us.

CHAPTER THREE

Parts Work and Conflict

The key characteristic of culturally mature perspective is that it reveals the inherent limitations of ideological worldviews. Put in Parts Work terms, it highlights how ideologic conflicts reflect parts arguing with parts and how ideological advocacy is a product of parts taking over and talking to the world. Here we see how Parts Work can begin to address not only personal psychological concerns, but also some of the social/political issues that define our time.

Understanding conflict in this way has a particularly immediate kind of pertinence in our time as conflict between ideological factions has often become so pronounced that real conversation about a great many topics has become largely impossible. Extreme polarization is setting neighbor against neighbor, creating distraction that gets in the way of addressing essential questions, and often putting us at great risk.

These circumstances highlight an essential recognition both for getting beyond today's knee-jerk polar animosities and for understanding how Cultural Maturity's changes might provide an antidote. In the end, ideology has less to do with what we think than how we think. Ultimately it is about something more basic even than collections of beliefs and values, what people refer to with a term like "worldview"—though that gets us a bit closer. At its most fundamental, ideology is about psychological patterns: It is not so much that belief creates polarization than it is that polarity's role in how we think creates polarized belief. Parts Work engages those psychological patterns directly.

Bill and Environmental Decision-Making

I cite this example, which also appears in my book, *Creative Systems Theory*, because it provides a concise place to start. While it draws on only a couple of parts, it captures the way Parts Work can readily shift between personal concerns and larger cultural issues. The example comes from individual therapy with a fifty-year-old respected biologist and environmentalist. I will call him Bill.

The immediate reason Bill had come to see me was depression that followed the death of this father. But with time, Bill recognized a further concern—what he described as a war within himself.

Bill's father had left him a beautiful piece of land that had been in the family for generations. He loved the place and planned to construct a cabin and move there when he retired. However, because of new zoning regulations that had made the land unbuildable, suddenly his plans were on hold. He felt deeply sad—and angry. But even more disturbing than the situation was the way his response to it had torn him from a comfortable set of beliefs. He was known for banging heads with property rights proponents, and often emerging victorious. Now, disparate internal voices were advocating not just different social policies, but contradictory views of the world. Distressed and confused by this conflict, Bill asked if we could somehow explore it.

While I recognized that such work would present some difficulties, I agreed. Bill was an exceptionally intelligent man with well thought-out beliefs that were not easily challenged. If I was to be of help, we would have to do more than just talk.

I began by having Bill imagine his two warring parts—the "environmentalist" and the "property rights advocate"—as if they were two actors on a stage. I asked him to describe everything he could about each character—what it wore, its age, the expression on its face. Then I had him invite them into the room. The environmentalist sat down on stage left:

sensitive features, longish hair. The property rights advocate stood further away with arms crossed, stage right: stocky build, a baseball cap tucked under his arm. After a bit, he too sat down.

I instructed Bill to turn to the two figures and describe the issue he wanted to address. After a bit of initial self-consciousness, he proceeded to talk with them about the land, the new regulations, and the deep conflict he felt. Then I suggested that he approach each chair and speak as that character—"become" it and give voice to what it felt about the questions at hand. I instructed Bill to return to his own chair after each character had said its piece and from there to respond to the chair that had spoken, and to follow up with any further questions. I offered that he should let himself be surprised by what each character might say.

This back and forth went through multiple iterations, first Bill speaking, then, in turn, each of the parts. The character in the chair to his left spoke of the importance of protecting the environment in its natural state. The character to his right argued that the government was wrong to dictate what a person did with private property. Both expressed a longing to live in the beautiful place. As the dialogue progressed and Bill's relationships with each of them deepened, he became increasingly able to find a place in himself where he could both respect what each character had to say and see limits to its helpfulness.

After some time, Bill turned to me and said he felt a bit disoriented, but that the conversation had helped. Both surprised and moved by much of what the two characters said, he found it particularly enlightening that each character seemed well-intentioned. Having framed the environmental vs. property rights conflict as a battle between good and ignorance (if not worse) we discussed how it was more accurately a battle between competing goods. Initially he struggled with resisting the environmentalist; but, with time, he recognized that in fact each character had important things to say.

While this work hadn't solved Bill's dilemma surrounding the property issue, it had given him a more solid place to stand for making decisions. He had begun to see a more complete picture that offered at least the potential for more creative choices.

Later I asked Bill if the exercise might have broader implications for his professional efforts, and we decided to continue with the hands-on approach. Confronted with particularly thorny questions that pitted environmental advocacy against property rights concerns, his task was to use his two "consultants," the environmentalist and the property-rights advocate, to help him determine the most effective and fair approach from the perspective of his Whole-Person chair. The result in each case was a deeper understanding of the dilemmas involved and, in several instances, novel solutions.

In fact, Parts Work almost always involves more parts than just two. And it often takes several months of work before a person can sit solidly in the Whole-Person (whole-box-of-crayons, Integrative Meta-perspective) chair. But this example illustrates a general approach that is both straightforward and effective.

The Abortion Debate

Abortion is another issue where we find extreme polarization. Certainly opinions divide along party lines; but because the abortion question splits people into opposing camps so quickly, it warrants our attention.

Consulting work I did a few years back with a social services organization illustrates how Parts Work can at least provide a place to start. Abortion had become a hot-button issue in the organization, and contentious feelings were getting in the way of people working together. I often use the same general kind of Parts Work approach with groups, particularly with those that are experiencing internal conflicts or dealing with controversial issues.

When working in this way, I start by having individuals or small subgroups represent the competing voices. A second group, sitting separately, assumes the role of the Whole-Person/Whole-System chair, and these people are given a sequence of tasks. First, to clarify the divergent positions, they engage the advocate groups in conversation. They then talk among themselves, seeking larger ways of thinking. And finally, they attempt to articulate conclusions and describe how these larger ways of understanding might translate into right and timely action.

Working with the social services organization in which abortion had become a contentious issue, I began by separating out two small groups: one to speak for the pro-life position and the other for pro-choice. To make things more interesting, each group had to argue the position opposite that which they held. Other people who held those positions served as consultants to the advocates, helping them make effective arguments. The rest of the participants were tasked with finding larger perspective; they sat in a circle outside the advocate groups.

To start the process, the two small groups spoke in turn, with the consultants coaching the advocates on the important points. The main arguments were those we commonly hear: The pro-life group argued that abortion was murder while the pro-choice group countered that the decision should rest with the woman (or the woman and her doctor).

Next I invited people in the outer circle to ask curiosity questions that would clarify positions (the process allowed no debate at this point). While this helped fill out understanding, it failed to alter the conversation. The positions of the two groups remained mutually exclusive.

The people in the outer circle then attempted to discuss the issue systemically, quietly in pairs; and after a time shared their conclusions. While their efforts didn't provide final answers, their reflections did move the conversation from a debate about right and wrong to interactions that acknowledged legitimate feelings on both sides.

Several contributions proved particularly useful in this regard. A man who leaned more pro-choice offered that he found it impossible to escape that abortion was in fact a kind of killing—that at the least it was the ending of a potential life. He apologized to his pro-choice colleagues, acknowledging that they might not be happy with his conclusion. But he quickly went on to suggest that denying this reality was only hiding from the real question and made real conversation impossible. And in the end, it simply left out what he felt was an essential fact.

A woman who leaned more pro-life also apologized, observing that, while what she had to say helped her, others might find it too philosophical. She described how she found herself questioning whether death was the right way to think about the opposite of life and struggled to find words to express a better way of thinking about it. Eventually she proposed that, instead of being pro-life in a literal sense, perhaps people needed to think in terms of what most ultimately honored life. And while she wasn't quite sure what she meant, she also offered that being sure that life endured might not be the only way to do so. Several of her colleagues countered that such semantics accomplished nothing—that death could not be consistent with life; but the observation did invite people to stretch their assumptions.

Conversations continued for about an hour, going back and forth between the two advocacy groups and the people tasked with finding a larger picture. Rarely was there full agreement, but the stated goal—of generating greater mutual respect—was gradually achieved. People were able to get to the place where productive conversation at least became possible.

I often use the abortion debate to illustrate an important principle. Almost any time polarized belief manifests in a specifically moral quandary, we assume that we must choose between good and evil. But if a question is indeed a good-versus-evil issue, it is not a quandary, for it is obvious what we need to do: the good. Rather, moral quandaries juxtapose competing goods. Clearly this is the case with the abortion debate, which pits the sanctity of life against a woman's right to choose. Each is clearly a good—and an important kind of good.

This principle could provide a beginning to reframing the abortion debate, but people aren't used to thinking in terms of competing goods. And the task is further compounded by a circumstance that we commonly find with thorny issues: Each position advocates for a very different kind of good. Caught with such apples-and-oranges considerations, we confront major difficulties not just because different people may value one good as opposed to the other. Because we are dealing with wholly different concerns, there is no way we can meet halfway even if we were inclined to. Parts Work suggests a way to at least move a step closer, though it can help only if a person is ready for this level of reflection.

Stephen and the Immigration Debate

Stephen was in his mid-forties, sat on his town's city council, and was a respected member of his community. I'd already seen Stephen for several months when he came in following the Thanksgiving holidays looking concerned. As his family spanned the extremes politically, the dinner table conversation had become quite heated.

Debate around the immigration question had left Stephen feeling particularly disturbed. Stephen's uncle was very conservative and left no doubt that he thought immigration should be severely restricted. Stephen's sister felt just as strongly that immigration benefited the country and that making citizenship possible for people from other countries was the only moral thing to do, particularly where circumstances in their native countries were troubled. Neither Stephen's uncle nor his sister were willing to back down.

As Stephen described the scene, I asked him what about the dinner table conversation had most bothered him. At first he thought the answer to my question was obvious—no one would find that degree of conflict in a family a good thing. But with reflection, he saw that his reaction was personal. As Stephen realized that he didn't have good answers for the immigration question, the issue evoked a similar kind of conflict in himself. Indeed, he had little of great use to say about the topic. He could feel his stomach begin to hurt when he thought about it. Given his role on the city council, this was not a small matter. He would clearly need to spend more time with the question and discover better ways to think about it than he had found thus far.

After I described how Parts Work provided a simple way to address controversial issues, Stephen agreed to give it a try. The first part Stephen identified was very much like his uncle—indeed, so much so that Stephen felt embarrassed to own it as a part of himself. It wore a cowboy hat and bordered on being overtly racist. Stephen gave it a chair to his right.

At least initially, Stephen felt more comfortable with the second part that he identified, a college professor who held views more like those of his sister. But as Stephen got more in touch with this second part, he found himself questioning its conclusions as well. The professor's views seemed too pat, even arrogant.

In preparation for engaging the parts, Stephen and I talked further about the Parts Work approach. After sharing the cardinal rules, I pointed out that parts in him apparently had been talking to other parts. I suggested that the pain Stephen felt in his stomach was likely a symptom of this internal tension. Stephen's first task would be to cut the "wire" between the parts, so they would talk only directly to him. His second task would be to talk with each part to find out what it had to contribute and the value of what each had to offer.

As Stephen went back and forth multiple times, talking first with one part and then the other, he began to appreciate that the immigration question was legitimately complex and that the values expressed by each part were in their own ways valid. Each reflected a kind of good. His "cowboy" part, while concerned with pride of place and the importance of protecting community and heritage, also wanted to be sure there would be good jobs for people's children. It sounded scared and angry that what many people had worked hard for might be taken away. On the other hand, the professor part also voiced values that Stephen could get behind. It described the U.S. as a country of immigrants and how our differences made us strong. It proposed that immigration was good for the economy, not the reverse, and made the same moral argument that Stephen's sister had voiced: that welcoming people in need was the compassionate thing to do.

But as Stephen spoke with the parts, it also became clear to him that each in its own way missed the mark. Both left out important pieces of the puzzle and reached conclusions that were problematic and sometimes simply wrong. For example, at one point the more conservative part argued that immigration puts us in danger because immigrants are often criminals—an observation that Stephen knew was not supported by evidence. With similar conviction, the liberal part talked as if open borders was the answer—a conclusion that Stephen knew came no closer to the truth and was just as dangerous.

At one point, I asked Stephen if his Parts Work conversations were proving helpful. His first response was to express disappointment that not much had changed. He felt no closer to an answer for the immigration question—indeed, in some ways, he felt further away. At least his parts were sure of their convictions. Talking with them had left him with an impossibly complex picture of potential benefits and possible detriments of immigration.

But I disagreed, offering that, while Stephen had yet to derive much that could help at the level of policy, I saw important change. Wasn't he seeing things more clearly, finding it easier to take everything into account that needed to be considered? He agreed that he was. When asked how his stomach was doing, to his surprise, he found that it felt considerably better.

As we talked further, I shared an experience that helped me frame the immigration debate more usefully. A colleague in Europe had contacted me angrily after reading an article I had written on immigration policy. After a dramatic influx of immigrants into his town had overwhelmed social services, and, in his view, left little of the town's tradition and history intact, he regretted his previous liberal feelings about immigration. While I felt moved by what my colleague said, I recognized how different the circumstances were in the state of Washington where I live. Here, the consequences of immigration have been almost entirely positive. We would not have either an apple industry or a high-tech industry—industries central to the state's economy and identity—without the contributions of immigrants. My colleague and I were deeply struck by the dramatic effect of context on the immigration question.

After describing this experience to Stephen, I also shared an image that helped me think about the immigration question more contextually: that of a cell's outer membrane. Without a strong outer membrane, a cell's life would be impossible. At the same time, it is just as critical that the membrane be permeable, to let in essential nutrients. The cell's task is to discern the relationship of solidity and permeability that is just right at particular times and places.

Stephen found the cell membrane image useful in that it facilitated a systemic understanding; certainly it helped him better appreciate how there was no one-size-fits-all answer with immigration. But it also helped him understand that it was possible to arrive at "good enough" answers in particular contexts. Stephen saw that his task, if he was to provide leadership for the town council, would be to help its members discern a balance—the right degree and kind of permeability—for the town's specific circumstances.

I suggested that Stephen again turn to his parts and articulate his new approach—to make an internal "leadership statement." He clarified his task as making this more nuanced kind of discernment and said he felt each of them had important contributions to make towards achieving this task, each of them being a valuable consultant.

Stephen then had an additional, equally important insight: He saw that he would need more than two parts if he was to make effective decisions; he needed to add parts that voiced everything that went into creating healthy and vibrant communities. Over the ensuing months, Stephen's Parts Work helped him to find greater equanimity in himself as well as to be more effective and comfortable in his leadership role with the city council.

CHAPTER FOUR

Parts Work and Relationship

In Chapter Two, we saw how Parts Work helps us understand how identity changes in a culturally mature reality. Our ideas of what it meant to be a person in times past were based on identification with parts and the relationships between those parts—a strong vs. a weak part, for instance. In contrast, Whole-Person identity draws on a more conscious and encompassing experience of Self: one based on holding and taking responsibility from the whole of one's multifaceted complexity.

Just as important is how Parts Work can help us understand changes reshaping relationships. Historically, relationships have been based on the projection of parts, most noticeably in the case of romantic love. By projecting masculine or feminine parts of ourselves onto another person, we've made that person into an idealized other half. We've seen something similar with leadership: By projecting our authority onto leaders, we gained the comforting purity of a mythologized picture of determination. Similarly, "two-halves-make-a-whole" dynamics typically have modeled our experience of parenting and friendship.

The concept of Cultural Maturity proposes that we become increasingly capable of Whole-Person bonds. Parts Work offers a concrete way to understand the needed changes; and, in the process, clarifies how Whole-Person relationship is different from what we have known. Whole-Person relationship is about loving and leading from the whole of who we are in ways that consciously draw on the whole of our complex natures.

Michelle and Whole-Person Intimacy

Michelle was in her mid-forties when she came to see me,. She described a pattern of abusive relationships that included two marriages—often physically abusive and always filled with conflict. Despite the abuse, she would stick with these relationships.

In her Parts Work, the first part Michelle identified was quiet and unassuming. When she spoke to the part, it seemed passive, even submissive in its responses, as if it were a fragile victim. But when that part took over Michelle felt more in control, if not more powerful.

These feelings began to make sense when Michelle described how her relationships usually progressed. Early on, the part would act helpless in ways that certain men would find attractive. These were not men that would ultimately be healthy for Michelle, but she saw that this was a kind of attraction she could count on.

As Michelle became more acquainted with this part, she began to understand her role in the conflict that had so often accompanied her relationships: Once a relationship began, this part would often undermine it, bringing out the worst in the already troubled men she had chosen to be with.

To her surprise, Michelle saw that there were ways in which the resulting conflict had often served her. Certainly it guaranteed that the men would not get too close, thereby keeping her safe. At the same time it brought excitement and protected Michelle from feeling alone. We observed that two people who are fighting never stop thinking about each other.

With these observations, Michelle began to have more insight into her past relationships—the forms they had taken and why she stayed, knowing they were not healthy.

Over time in our work together, Michelle became acquainted with other parts of herself: a creative part, an assertive part that encouraged her to stand up for herself, an intellectual part that expressed frustration that Michelle was not doing more with her life. Michelle began to explore what it would mean to live from her own Whole-Person chair more solidly. She practiced setting boundaries for the part that had so often taken over. She also began to draw more consciously on all her parts in making life choices. When she did, although life was not as predictable, Michelle was coming to like herself more.

As far as men went, Michelle came to recognize that having a man always there for her had stopped being important in the same way. She also found herself attracted to men who in their own ways were more complete. Every now and then she missed the predictable excitement she had known in the past; but such feelings quickly passed as she recognized what more she had become.

Mark and Relationship Fears

For Mark, a man in his early thirties, relationships thus far in his life had rarely gone well. While they might have been quite close initially, after a month or so they would fall apart. He had yet to maintain a successful love relationship for any length of time. As he sat before me, he seemed unsure of himself and oddly distant.

After a few sessions to get acquainted, I introduced the concept of Parts Work. The first part Mark identified was a gruff old man who wasn't very open to talking, other than commenting that it really didn't like women that much (or the idea of therapy).

The second part had very different sentiments. Romantic to an extreme, it was not only attracted to women; it idealized them. Mark was fonder of this part and commented that it was probably the part that had gotten him to see me.

After we worked together over several weeks, a pattern became apparent. When Mark was initially attracted to a woman, the romantic part took charge. In effect, it was this part that was having the relationship. But within a short time, the gruff old man would intercede. When it did, the relationship would become increasingly conflicted and quickly come to an end. When the old man was in charge, Mark was clearly not a pleasant person to be around.

To go more deeply, I suggested that Mark talk with the old man part. Mark turned to it and asked pointedly, "What is your problem?" He then went over to its chair to hear what the part had to say.

"When you let the romantic part take over, you do stupid things. I'm trying to keep you safe," it said. Evidently the old man interfered for a good reason: He was protecting Mark from losing himself in what was, in essence, a limited connection.

Mark and I talked at length about what it might be like to relate to a woman from his Whole-Person chair rather than just the romantic part. At first the idea confused him. It seemed less interesting than his usual behavior, and he couldn't see why he would want to relate in this way. But he agreed to give it a try.

Over the ensuing weeks of Parts Work, Mark practiced communicating from a Whole-Person place. He found himself more willing to reach out to women and in general to relate to women in more caring ways. With time, he achieved the tangible reward of a new relationship that began to grow and endure in ways that relationships had not before.

When Mark later asked the gruff old man part what it thought of the new relationship, to his surprise it had no objection. Indeed, it liked that Mark had a woman in his life. Even more surprising, the old man no longer seemed so gruff—or so old.

As Mark continued his conversations with the old man part, it shared that in truth it had liked women all along. Its only problem was that Mark didn't seem to know how to have a relationship without sacrificing his own identity. The old man proposed that if Mark could love from his Whole-Person chair, he would not only be supportive of Mark having love in his life, but he would also be happy to help out in any way he could.

Helen and Parenting

Helen was thirty and the mother of two kids: a ten-year-old daughter and a six-year-old son. Her reason for coming, at least initially, was less for herself than for her son, Mikey, who was having trouble making friends at school, acting dependent and clingy with her, and still wetting his bed.

As we got to know each other in the first session, the focus quickly turned toward Helen. Putting it simply, she felt she had no idea how to parent a boy. Her daughter was doing fine; but she often felt conflicted and confused when it came to Mikey. Mikey's dad was in and out of the picture.

When we began doing Parts Work, I asked Helen which part seemed most related to her feelings with Mikey. She described a woman tightly clinging to her son, a kind of Madonna, all loving and ever-present. When asked how she felt about the part, Helen realized she was quite ambivalent toward it. While the part was loving, Helen suspected that its relationship with Mikey had more to do with itself than really seeing her son.

When I asked how it saw her son, Helen was afraid the part might be dismissive of Mikey; but, on the contrary, it made him too special. I offered that if this part was a Madonna, that Mikey was a bit like a Christ child. Helen recognized the important sense in which that was the case.

We discussed Whole-Person parenting and what parenting Mikey might look like from her Whole-Person chair rather than from that part. At first the question confused Helen, so I asked whether there were other parts in her that might contribute to parenting.

After thinking about it, she observed that there was another parent part, though she didn't like it. The second part was a helicopter mom, the kind of mom most concerned with getting her child into an Ivy League school. Helen knew a lot of parents like that and said that she wanted to be very sure she didn't become one of them.

As I continued to question Helen about other parts, she described one that was a good friend and community member; another that liked to work in the garden; and the part that used to have an intimate relationship with her husband.

Upon seeing an uncomfortable look come over her face with that last recognition, I asked her what she was feeling. She had seen that in important ways her son was replacing her husband: In making Mikey the Christ child she was giving the kind of attention to him that she had given to her husband when their connection had felt romantic and new. Obviously, this was not the kind of attention that Mikey needed.

We retuned to discussing the Whole-person relationship, this time more broadly. I observed that she might want to revisit her relationship with her husband from her Whole-Person chair instead of from that one part. It was a topic that helped Helen greatly.

But the more immediate question was how she could better parent Mikey. I had her address her parts with a leadership statement, making it clear that, from here forward, she alone would be doing the parenting. She set clear boundaries for both the Madonna part and the romantic part.

At this point I suggested that all her parts could contribute to her being a Whole-Person parent. This suggestion surprised Helen; but when she saw how it could help her, she began brainstorming with her parts about different parenting situations that she had found confusing. Oddly the friend and gardener part were often particularly helpful. Helen knew her job was not just to be her son's friend. But the matter-of-factness the parts brought to their parenting discussions helped Helen get beyond her tendency to make her son something more than he was. She had to set a strong boundary for the helicopter mom part; but she let it contribute as long as it didn't get in the way of Mikey's growing autonomy. And the same was true even of the Madonna part, which was ultimately a loving part. But with each conversation, it became clearer that none of these parts had a relationship with Mikey. They could be consultants to her in her parenting, but no more than that.

As Helen dove deeper into her personal work, she came to recognize what it was she ultimately wanted for her son. She wanted him to be his own person, able to sit in his own Whole-Person chair and make his life choices according to the things that most mattered to him. She also saw that her way of parenting, making him "special" and seeming to support such an outcome, in fact was having the opposite effect. Her therapy was making her a more authentically loving person, all the way around.

Henry and Whole-Person Leadership

I was surprised when Henry, a fifty-one-year old surgeon and department head in a large hospital, came to therapy. Given his time of life, I thought it might be issues with his marriage, or perhaps midlife depression, that brought him to see me.

In fact, what he wanted to explore was how he could be a better leader. When one of the younger physicians under him had confronted him and challenged his leadership style, it was clear that at the very least Henry needed to be a better listener, with both his patients and his young residents. And he sensed that there were deeper reasons why some self-examination might be in order.

Parts Work is a great fit for such general reflection, so we dove right in. Henry brought a handful of parts into the room, the most prominent being a very professional part, which wore a white coat. Another part was more philosophical, and another wore waders, dressed for fishing, as Henry loved to fish. A fourth part had the concerned look of a psychologist or social worker.

When I asked Henry where he wanted to start, he began to share more about his young colleague's observation. But part way through he stopped and made an important observation. While in his life as whole he drew on all of these parts, when he stepped into his role as head of the surgery department, he became only the part in the white coat. This part, while very intelligent and competent, lacked people skills.

With this recognition, Henry responded with satisfaction that he now understood the work we needed to do: help that part become a more sensitive leader. To his surprise, I disagreed. I suggested that the task would be more complex than that, while at the same time there were ways in which it would be simpler.

I explained how our medical training had supported that white-coat part taking charge: The long hours on call in the emergency room; leading from a this place of absolute authority, given the responsibility and uncertainty inherent to the profession; making life-and-death decisions every day.

I also talked about the changing needs of leadership in our time and the importance of Whole-Person leadership, which drew on more of himself. While the changes might often appear subtle, I explained, they were fundamental, and included how he carried himself as a physician, how he made decisions, and how he related to both patients and colleagues. And these changes would require confronting his responsibilities and uncertainties with a new directness.

Henry generally grasped what I was saying. Indeed, his first response was to say that he thought I was describing the kind of deeper change that he had sensed he was seeking. But he also looked puzzled as to what that might involve and how to go about getting there. It all sounded a bit overwhelming.

I offered that it was here that the task became simpler. In Parts Works terms, he needed to learn how to be a more effective physician and leader from his Whole-Person chair, and that was something we could do simply by practicing.

Such practice defined the larger part of the next six months of our work together. Henry would bring up an issue from the week before; and, using his parts as consultants, he would explore how to address it. With each session he gained new skills and sensitivities, and each part had things to contribute. Initially, the psychological part added the most by helping him be more attentive to others and sensitive to their needs. But the philosophical part helped ease his discomfort with some of the more unsettling needed changes. Interestingly, the fisherman part had a particularly important role to play, encouraging him to be more down-to-earth in his interactions, less often the "expert," and, when appropriate, just a person. To his surprise, Henry learned that when the white-coated part wasn't in charge, he could draw even more effectively on its expertise.

Most important, over those six months, Henry was getting increasingly comfortable and adept at leading from his Whole-Person chair. Increasingly it became common sense.

One topic proved particularly significant for Henry: the topic of death. The work he had done to that point was more than personal in that the kind of leadership Henry was learning was the needed, more complete sort that the concept of Cultural Maturity describes. But when he confronted the subject of death specifically, Henry entered culturally mature territory with a directness that he had not before encountered.

It happened when the philosophical part confronted Henry with what it felt was a blind spot: Modern medicine was rooted in a heroic mythology where death and disease were seen as enemies to be defeated. The part observed that, when Henry gave the white-coated part power to be in charge, he tended to keep death at arm's length.

Henry had to admit that he often had a difficult time talking to patients about death and answering his residents' death-related questions. Had this at times led to unnecessary and unhelpful care? At the least it may have kept Henry from considering all the options.

At my suggestion, from his Whole-Person chair Henry engaged all his parts about death and its implications, putting questions of responsibility and uncertainty inescapably in the forefront.

Henry talked with his parts about the importance of making death always a legitimate topic and asked their advice about how this might be accomplished. During this dialog he also examined how unnecessary care not only increased costs but also often led to unnecessary suffering; and he led internal conversations about hospice care's role and how best to make use of it.

The topic of physician-assisted suicide proved especially challenging, placing his parts at odds. The white-coated surgeon held the traditional view that it violated the Hippocratic Oath, while the psychological part took the opposing position that people had a basic right to end their lives if they so chose. The philosophical part observed that at least we were dealing with an example of competing goods.

From his chair, Henry found the topic hard to get a handle on. While acknowledging that the growing acceptance of physician-assisted suicide was basically a good thing, he worried what could happen when there weren't adequate safeguards. He talked with his parts about recent legislation in Canada that made assisted suicide legal not only for patients with terminal physical ailments but also for those in pain; and, of particular concern, where psychiatric issues came into play. He wondered if inadequacies in our healthcare system would result in people making choices they otherwise would not.

One result of these reflections was an important conversation between Henry and me about culturally mature perspective and what it could accomplish from the vantage of that Whole-Person chair. We observed that, while it doesn't provide final truths, it offers that we hold the larger complexity of whatever needed to be considered. And it didn't save him from responsibility and uncertainty: Indeed, it made those challenges even more inescapable and fundamental. But it did offer that he could now better tolerate and learn from them.

CHAPTER FIVE

Parts Work and Big-Picture Questions

Parts Work, just by its nature, engages questions on the edge of current understanding. Sometimes it is our intent to take on such concerns; but often we end up there because it follows from the way the method works.

This chapter's Parts Work examples introduce questions that take us into new territory. The first touches on the often Janus-faced implications of technological advancement. The second highlights how culturally mature truth differs from spiritual truth. The third engages the changing realities of gender. And the fourth takes on a particularly encompassing cultural concern, the importance in our time of rethinking wealth and progress.

Stephanie and the Technological

When Stephanie first came to see me she was twenty-three and had just finished her first year at a major high-tech company after completing a degree in computer science. She described feeling a lot of pride as a woman having entered what has been a male-dominated field and found her new work intellectually stimulating. But at the same time she didn't like that her job wasn't making a difference in the world; indeed, she feared that ultimately it might produce more harm than benefit. And the fact that she had just become a parent was causing her to question some of her past choices.

Accordingly, Stephanie felt she had some big decisions to make. Her feelings that she might have chosen the wrong profession increasingly haunted her. And her doubts about being able to make a difference there were only part of it.

Unlike many people who had excelled educationally in STEM fields (Science, Technology, Engineering, and Math), Stephanie had broad interests that included the humanities, which often eclipsed her interest the sciences. Given how well the job paid, and having seen colleagues unable to escape the "golden handcuffs," she feared that if she stayed with her current work too long it would be hard to leave. She wondered if being a teacher or a psychologist—or even an anthropologist or archeologist, as those fields had always fascinated her—might be a better fit for her values. She also felt that, if she was going to make a change, now was the time to do it, while in her early years.

Parts Work was an ideal approach for the kind of questions that Stephanie was asking—questions about values, priorities, and life direction. The method came easily for her and she soon had six parts arranged around her in the room: a feminist; an engineer whose interests lay with the technological; a parent; a part with concerns about health (she regularly did yoga and was attentive to her diet); a part that found particular fascination in other cultures; and a part that she had to admit was rather a Luddite and had questioned her career choice from the beginning.

Stephanie began by simply asking the group whether her profession was a good fit. There was a lot of back and forth, and even though over the ensuing months Stephanie would learn a lot about herself, she wasn't arriving at an answer.

At one point I asked Stephanie to be more specific about her concerns with her field, and I observed that the Whole-Person chair had some capacities that could be helpful in this regard, particularly in grappling with competing goods. It would also help her to see limitations and to assess risks and dangers.

Realizing that her question ultimately was less about her specific job than about technological advancement in general, Stephanie identified three concerns: Many of the issues she most cared about did not have technological solutions; inadequate attention was given to the cost of new technologies; and "techno-utopian" assumptions were keeping people from recognizing real and important dangers. I suggested that Stephanie probe these three concerns more deeply with her parts.

Regarding the first concern, Stephanie's conversations with her parts confirmed what she had sensed: that in our time, we tended to assume that all our problems could be solved by technology. But the issues that most worried Stephanie—poverty, the extinction of species, and what appeared to be increasing discord in the world— required changes in values and priorities, regardless of technological innovations. Even an issue like climate change, where new technologies could play a major role, ultimately comes down to whether we are willing to make hard choices.

The second concern, that of runaway costs of technology, didn't provide the same depth of insight, but Stephanie felt it was important to take time with it. She emphasized that being cognizant of economic limits was important to getting our human priorities right—and her parts agreed. One topic that came up was going to Mars. Stephanie realized that she was much less willing than her more technologically-minded colleagues to consider it a good use of resources. While the project could be scientifically fascinating, the idea that it could provide an escape from problems on Earth seemed to Stephanie silly at best.

The third concern, technology's potential dangers, brought Stephanie closer to home. We agreed that unintended consequences of new digital technologies were of great concern. I offered that, as a psychiatrist, one of my greatest worries was that addictive dynamics were robbing people of their attention. We discussed how the long term results could be catastrophic and that there was no obvious way to avoid this kind of outcome. Stephanie's conversations with her parts around this concern contained rich and nuanced points about competing goods and real risks that needed to be taken more seriously.

It was many months before Stephanie returned to the more specific question of her life's direction and again threw the question out to her parts. Initially she was surprised at the extent to which the act of taking time to explore her concerns had deepened the inner conversation, and the direction the conversation ultimately took. Given the depth of these concerns, Stephanie expected her parts to want her to move on, to change her profession. Instead, the conversation emphasized how Stephanie's skills and awareness made her particularly good at understanding the human and moral dimensions of technological questions. Might that not be the place where she could make the greatest contribution with her life?

This insight would prove to be the essential missing piece. Stephanie was eventually assigned to a position at her company where she oversaw efforts to recognize risks and address the social implications of the company's efforts.

Anne and Spiritual Unity Fallacies

In Chapter One, I used the polarity between science and religion to illustrate how Parts Work can provide insight into big-picture questions. One implication was that culturally mature truth is different from both religious truth and scientific truth as we customarily think of them. The following example starts with a personal concern; but ultimately it brings attention not only to how spiritual truths and culturally mature differ, but also to significant implications of understanding how they do.

Anne came to see me less for therapy than for help in her role as a leader; but the work ended up being deeply demanding and transformative for her at a personal level. If she had known in advance where it would go, I doubt she would have begun.

About a year previous, Anne had been hired as the director of a local growth center, whose work focused primarily on New Age self-help and social change concerns. Anne was excited about the role. It gave her a chance to advocate for values that she cared about and to be seen as effective by others.

But there was one area where she was not effective. It had to do with one person in the organization who was problematical. This person had been with the growth center from its beginnings and was very influential; but she had a remarkable ability to undermine the efforts of other people. Something needed to be done, and Anne was the person who would have to do it.

But it soon became obvious that Anne was not prepared for this kind of situation; and, just as important, there was a good chance that the organization could not tolerate her taking the needed steps. Anne's Parts Work made both realities starkly apparent.

She began by bringing a variety of parts into the room: an artistic part, a naturalist part, a good friend part, a rational part, a practical part, and a meditator/spiritual part. I gave her time to learn about each part, and she found journaling helpful to deepen her understandings.

As we began work on Anne's leadership challenge, she found it difficult to talk at length about the problematical person. She assumed there was a way to change things so that she would stop being such an issue. And she expected that I could tell her how. But the more she described the situation, the more it seemed obvious that the kind of change she was hoping for was not an option.

Anne needed to set a major boundary—she needed to fire that person. In time, she recognized that this was the case, but she had a hard time facing this reality, frightened of how others would react. We dove deeper into Parts Work to see if we could find the needed perspective and necessary capacities.

I asked Anne what parts she would need to draw on to take the needed steps. She saw that the assistance of the rational part and the practical part could certainly help, but she was clearly uncomfortable with even beginning to talk with these parts about what might be required. These were not parts she was used to applying this explicitly, and it was apparent that other parts had problems with them as well.

Anne's discomfort with engaging these parts became evident in the following weeks as she kept coming up with excuses for missing her sessions. When we finally did get together again, I asked her which parts had found our previous conversations scary.

She offered that it seemed to be the meditative/spiritual part. Of particular importance, it became clear as we talked that Anne had a very difficult time distinguishing herself from this part. She described it as her essence, as the core of herself. As we talked it became clear that she valued the growth center because its purpose was to further this kind of sensibility. Anne had a hard time recognizing that this feature was only a part, and she had just as hard a time seeing how there could be anything wrong with this part running the show. Arguably she had shaped her whole life around advocating for this kind of result.

Anne was in a double bind. She needed to set a boundary and lead the organization to appreciate the need for this boundary. But the part she most associated with truth identified with spiritual oneness and the absence of boundaries. Therefore to be an effective leader would require a major cognitive change in herself: She had to stop identifying with the meditation/spiritual part and recognize it as only a part—albeit a powerfully important part, but ultimately only a part.

With this realization Anne once again disappeared, this time for several months. It was not clear to her that she could make the change in herself I had described; but it was clear to me that she wasn't sure she wanted to. Anne did realize that firing the person, who had become even more of a problem, was necessary, and she wanted my help in strategizing how best to do this.

I responded by telling a story from a few decades earlier, when I was part of an arts organization that was deeply valued by those involved. A person with a rather toxic personality had joined the organization, but no one would talk about it except behind closed doors. Eventually, because no one spoke up, it destroyed the organization (although I suspect the organization might not have survived even if someone had). The personalities of those in the organization were so uncomfortable with setting boundaries that the group's bonds would have been irreparably harmed had they taken the needed action. As with Anne's spiritual organization, the individuals in the arts organization identified with their "oneness" part rather than their Whole-Person perspective. When that is the case, the capacity for separation and boundaries needed for the healthy working of an organization can be nearly impossible to appreciate.

The story made Anne uncomfortable. As a leader, she recognized the double bind she was in: While the organization required that she set a boundary, it might not survive anyway.

The personal challenge might be even more fundamental, since her whole sense of purpose was tied to identifying with those meditative/spiritual parts as truth. To lead the organization from her Whole-Person self would be hard enough; she realized it would be even more of a challenge within herself.

I wish I could say this story had a happy ending. Perhaps it did, but I don't know because Anne again disappeared and this time didn't get back in touch. I know that several years later the growth center went out of business. More personally for Anne, I know that when it comes to Cultural Maturity, making the step beyond identifying with spiritual ideologies can be one of the most difficult. I hope things went well for her.

Jon and Gender Complexities

Jon was twenty-two when he first came to me for therapy. He described having had a rough adolescence, often feeling confused and depressed, and several times had attempted suicide. He had a hard time making friends, and being a friend to himself.

When I asked Jon to be more specific about his confused feelings, it became clear that he had conflicted feelings about gender. At times he fit in with the other guys, but as often he felt more connected with the girls. When he was alone, he would often imagine he was a girl.

This left him feeling torn inside, that there must be something deeply wrong with him; he couldn't imagine that anyone else might feel like this. His suicide attempts had followed times when his imaginings had been particularly strong.

The major reason that Jon had come to see me was that talking openly about gender was becoming more acceptable. Rather than just feeling bad about himself, he was beginning to feel curious, and he recognized that there were some important decisions he needed to make. Feeling sexually attracted to both women and men, he didn't know whether he wanted to live in the world as a man or as a woman—or, given today changing realities, something else.

Parts Work seemed a good fit for the questions Jon wanted to explore, and he quite readily brought a whole family of diverse parts into the room. In asking how he felt about them, he offered that they seemed "a rather crazy-quilt lot." Many of the parts couldn't be more different. He spent several sessions just getting to know them.

Later, in response to my asking Jon to be more specific about those differences, he observed that there were really two families of parts, one masculine, the other feminine. I've observed how parts often exist in polar relationships, but the way all his parts were split up this way was unusual. It was less that the groups were in conflict than that they seemed to exist in different worlds.

I could see that this recognition was affecting Jon deeply. He shared how it helped him make sense of a lot of the confusion he had experienced in growing up. It was like the groups were going back and forth as far as which one would be in charge. This would have been confusing enough if the two groups merely had either masculine or feminine characteristics. But it seemed that each group also had different ideas about whether Jon should think of himself as a man or a woman.

At first, this recognition only threw Jon back into the old confusions and self-doubt. But by engaging Jon in his Whole-Person chair, he was able to step back and begin to find curiosity in what he was discovering. We had a lengthy conversation about how most people's parts existed in polar relationships and how these polar relationships tended to juxtapose more archetypally masculine and archetypally feminine qualities. I noted that in his case the distinction was particularly pronounced, but that there was an important sense in which everyone was "non-binary." The observation at least helped Jon feel less alone—and less broken.

I talked with Jon about what it might mean to make choices from his chair rather than letting either group be in charge, and over the months that followed he practiced doing so. He also further explored each of the parts and his relationship with them. As he did so, he described a growing sense of strength and purpose in his life and a found fascination with just how complex one's inner life can be.

One aspect of his work surprised me: I had expected that, as he engaged his inner complexities from his Whole-Person chair, he would find a greater sense of integration. Leading from his chair gave him a more solid sense of identity and allowed him to hold and appreciate that inner complexity. But a year into working together, the two "families" he had initially described seemed as far apart as ever.

This outcome yielded an important consequence. I had expected that the decisions Jon had described as necessary as we were getting started would have emerged almost by themselves; that answers would become self-evident as Jon came to hold his inner complexity not only more consciously, but as an integrated whole. But this was not the case. Jon would be able to use his relationship with his parts to address those decisions, but doing so would be a different kind of challenge.

Over the next year, Jon took them on. The work to that point had at least made it possible for Jon to address them from a self-accepting—indeed loving—way. One thing Jon came to recognize was that they were different kinds of questions for him. Sexually, he realized that his feelings for both men and women were valid and important. He would think of himself as bisexual. With regard to gender, Jon found himself increasingly leaning in the direction of identifying as a woman. He recognized that it would be some time before he was fully confident in this decision, but he began to explore calling himself "Jonna" and dressing overtly as a woman.

Robert and Rethinking Profit

Robert was a forty-five-year-old financial analyst who had worked for Goldman Sacks for ten years when he came to see me. Having been divorced five years earlier, he described himself as going through a classic midlife crisis, wondering whether global finance was a good fit for him and questioning the integrity of his work.

As we talked, I found myself increasingly thinking either that Robert was selling himself short with his mid-life crisis interpretation, or at least that his interpretation needed to be placed in larger context. Worried that much of his work was widening the gap between haves and have-nots on the planet and that his work's unquestioned support for globalization was somehow missing the mark, Robert's concerns were clearly as much about needed changes in the world as they were about Robert's relationship with himself.

However, we began at a more personal level: Robert needed to regain his sense of purpose in his life. When it comes to questions of purpose, Parts Work's approach is straightforward. Robert needed to bring all of his parts into the room and engage them as deeply as possible in what most mattered to them. It would be Robert's job to listen carefully and go where these conversations led him.

One place they took him was the recognition that his question had as much to do with the state of the planet as with his inner psychological state. But, while he made important progress examining his values and getting his everyday life choices in line with those values, the result was not the depth of purpose he had hoped for. He saw that he needed to be willing to engage in larger questions if his life was to be ultimately satisfying to him. He needed to feel that his life really contributed.

With this insight, Robert concluded that he should get out of finance. But when he talked with his parts, to his surprise that was not their solution. They challenged him to think more courageously and creatively about finance and to be more of a leader. Of particular importance, they emphasized that this would require leading from the values that most mattered to him.

Robert found his parts' response intriguing as well as startling. While it was not at all obvious to him what their advice specifically would look like, it also seemed right. A first striking implication was that he needed to start from square one. His old ways of thinking about the bottom line as the measure of his efforts—the relationship between wealth and progress—were obviously insufficient.

I offered that Parts Work might be able to help him here. Since he had already used Parts Work to get in touch with what created meaning in his life—what most created "personal wealth"—maybe he could use a similar approach to rethink wealth and progress more generally.

In fact, the method proved remarkably straightforward. Robert needed to hold the concepts of wealth and progress in ways that took into account benefits of every sort, including financial, social, and the greater well-being of the natural world. By opening up the question to all of his parts, Robert found himself increasingly able to think about advancement in more systemic ways. Many past assumptions had to fall away; but in the process, he found himself feeling a new excitement about what his contribution might be.

We applied this new measure of wealth to all manner of concerns that he had previously framed wholly in economic terms. Each time we did, his perspective expanded in ways that identified essential questions he had not previously considered. For example, he found himself rethinking his part's assumption that globalization was inherently good. Once this part came out as a strong advocate for local control, it emphasized how much was lost when mass culture erased local uniqueness. Robert saw that the part had a good point; but other parts were just as adamant that globalization had made important contributions.

Suddenly Robert realized that setting local against global, as we often see today in conservative versus liberal advocacy, wasn't helpful. He saw that we needed systemic models that could draw on and support the benefits inherent in each of these viewpoints. Such models would fundamentally redefine economics and require that we also think in new ways about government and its workings. In all this, Robert recognized a compelling question, one that might provide the purpose for his life he was hoping to find.

CHAPTER SIX

Further Reflections—Putting the Method in Context

Let's step back for some big-picture reflections on Parts Work's accomplishments and its implications for general understanding. I'll start by drawing on the examples from previous chapters to highlight where the method's power lies and reveal some of the recognitions that begin to become self-evident in doing Parts Work. I will then look more closely at Parts Work's place in the history of psychology and psychotherapy. Finally, I'll reflect on a handful of overarching questions, from the way Parts Work differs when used with people who have different styles, to what it can tell us about the ultimate nature of truth.

Where Its Power Lies

With each chapter I've illustrated the power of Parts Work by presenting a specific concern that it helped us address. Equally important is how, with each of these accomplishments, a particular aspect of culturally mature reality becomes self-evident.

Addressing Questions of Purpose

In multiple examples we recognized how Parts Work helps us address questions of purpose and direction in our lives. We saw this at a personal level in Tom's confrontation with our modern Crisis of Purpose; and its more collective implications were evident when Robert came face to face with the need in our time to rethink wealth and progress.

Note that a further essential implication from this recognition is that Parts Work supports the conclusion that purpose—particularly a creative kind of purpose—is inherent to being human. In our time, the responses of parts are reactive and predictable,[3] whereas choices made from Parts Work's Whole-Person chair are inherently generative.

Addressing Conflict

Through Dale's use of Parts Work to address anger and procrastination, we recognized how the method can help us reconcile inner conflicts. And with Rebecca, we saw Parts Work's power as a tool for getting beyond the separate-world realties of conflicting ideologies.

Equally important is Part Work's ability to support the simple yet profound recognition that a more encompassing reality, beyond polar conflicts, might exist. We can overlook this personally; and certainly, in today's world, where so many issues divide people into polar camps, it represents an essential—if not radical—realization.

Rethinking Relationship

In Chapter Four, by applying Parts Work to relationships of multiple sorts—Michelle's love relationships, Helen's parenting relationships, and Henry's leadership relationships—we saw how it can help solve relationship problems. We also saw how it points toward an evolution in how we think about and approach relationship: the possibility of relating more fully from the whole of who we are.

This new reality that becomes self-evident when doing relationship-related

---

[3] I say "in our time" because, in times past," crosstalk" has in fact been generative. Before the possibility of Integrative Meta-perspective, interactions between parts—for example between Left versus Right on the political stage or religion versus science—served to take us forward. Today, increasingly they leave us stuck in dead-end conversations.

Parts Work is the "new common sense" nature of Whole-Person relationship, a new step that is essential to relationships in our time. We also see that it is ultimately not that complicated: It is what relationship naturally becomes when we engage it from Parts Work's Whole-Person chair.

Rethinking Identity

The related insights we gain from identity-related Parts Work is consistent with what Creative Systems Theory calls the Myth of the Individual, which alerts us to the fact that we have never identified with the whole of ourselves: The projections of "two-halves-make-a whole" relationships leave us identifying only with singular aspects of who we are, making the whole idea of "self-concept" based on decidedly partial understandings of what it means to be a "self."

In contrast, identity as experienced from Parts Work's Whole-Person chair becomes wholly new, more complete. Importantly, we don't need to create it—it follows naturally from sitting in that chair. Neither do we need to understand it; indeed, it lies beyond our understanding. Reflecting the whole of our complexity, this identity engages a reality that cannot be captured with understanding as we conventionally think of it.

Realizing Systemic Perspective

We can capture all these results with the recognition that Parts Work propels us into a more systemic kind of reality. We saw this with Robert's dilemma about his career in finance, and how Parts Work offered him an understanding of moral questions in terms of competing goods. Similarly, Stephen found a more complete way of understanding the immigration question while addressing the issue from the Whole-Person chair.

Both of these observations imply an essential systems-related recognition.

However, the kind of systems thinking that comes naturally from the perspective of the Whole-person chair differs from the ways the word "systems" is most often used. It is neither just the systemic complexity of multi-faceted mechanical systems nor the "all is one" picture of connectedness associated with spiritual systems. With each of those we encounter the word "system" in reference to the perspective of only a particular part. In contrast, the recognition of the "procreative" symmetry that links parts points toward the larger, more life-acknowledging and generative kind of systemic understanding we have interest in.

Parts Work and Psychotherapy

I've proposed that Parts Work represents a major step forward in the practice of psychotherapy. This is not to say it doesn't have important antecedents. I've observed that there are other approaches that work actively with parts, most notably Fritz Perl's Gestalt therapy, Jacob Moreno's psychodrama, and Roberto Assagioli's psychosynthesis. We can also go back to modern psychiatry's beginnings for parallels, at least in how psychological dynamics are conceived. Sigmund Freud's id, ego, and superego can be thought of as general categories for parts, as can Carl Jung's anima, animus, self, and shadow. Jung's active imagination approaches stepped beyond the conceptual in inviting people to engage and manipulate symbolic elements.

But Parts Work is unique in supporting Cultural Maturity's cognitive reordering and the new capacities that Integrative Meta-perspective makes possible. To see how this is the case we can look to the three cardinal rules that define the Parts Work process. Together they support culturally mature understanding and growth in ways that other methods at best do only by inference.

Most immediately, only the Whole-Person Chair talks to the world, something not found with other methods. Also, only the person in the Whole-

Person leadership chair (not the therapist/facilitator) talks with parts, again something unique to the approach. The rule that parts don't talk to other parts similarly reflects an original contribution. Past notions of both psychodynamics and social/political dynamics were based on ways of thinking that were essentially parts talking to parts. The way Parts Work places the final authority not with the therapist as interpreter but in the hands of the person in the Whole-Person leadership chair might seem similar to humanistic methodologies; but because of the fundamental difference between that which the Whole-Person leadership chair represents and the way humanistic belief conceives of identity, again we are seeing something new.

Other observations that follow from applying the Parts Work method help fill out the importance of its contribution and bring refinement to the method. One such observation follows from the rule that only the Whole-Person chair talks to the world, and that includes the therapist. People often ask how transference in the classical sense is handled within Parts Work. It is addressed in Parts Work by acknowledging that, in the end, transference is simply a part believing it has a relationship with the therapist. Once the misplaced relationship is pointed out, the Whole-Person chair engages the part and sets the needed boundary.

Another observation concerns the prospect of changing a part that is being troublesome. The short answer is that it cannot be done—not, at least, by trying. Trying to change a part will only make it stronger; it will assume that because it is getting attention it must be doing something right. But in fact when parts do change, it is as a response to the right kind of leadership from the Whole-Person chair. The appropriate response in engaging a part is to make use of its input if it provides benefit and to ignore it if it does not. It all comes down to a simple question: Is the part being helpful or not helpful? Parts naturally want to be helpful, and if they are ignored, they will seek out ways to contribute. Engaged in this way, parts do change, and often in ways that are not only unexpected, but profound.

Another observation can be tricky to grasp, but it follows from the rule about parts and the world. It is not just that parts don't talk to the world, but that they have no relationship to the world. Often a person will find a part scanning the world to try to make sense of it or to provide protection. The person then needs to set a boundary and turn the part's attention back to where it belongs—on the actions and leadership of the Whole-Person chair. Helpful contributions from parts reflect how parts are feeling about that leadership.

A simple way to detect when a part is taking over is that, when addressed by the person in the Whole-Person chair, it responds as if it is the one having the experience. For example, instead of saying, "I think it would help if you were more assertive," it might say, "I need to be more assertive." Therefore, as people work through the method, one of the most common interventions I employ is to counsel that they listen to their pronouns.

Perhaps surprisingly, I tend to counsel people against giving their parts names, the simple reason being that, as the work deepens, parts grow and evolve. People can find names helpful, but labels can get in the way of change. Therefore it often works best to associate a part with a chair rather than a name.

If someone doesn't have a particular goal for a session, I will often suggest that the person ask the parts what they would like to talk about. The results with such sessions are often particularly powerful.

Parts Work alters not just how a person engages specific issues, but ultimately how the person engages experience as a whole. I've noted that one of the litmus tests for successful Parts Work is the appearance of culturally mature changes regarding concerns that have not been directly addressed.

Another interesting implication of Parts Work concerns the training of therapists, in that Parts Work requires special capacities. Certainly it requires an appreciation for culturally mature perspective and the ability to manifest it; but at the same time, much that is often seen as most important in the training of therapists becomes less pertinent. Parts Work requires a sensitivity to psychodynamics, but only rarely is it the therapist's job to interpret them. And while an appreciation for traditional notions of psychopathology can be valuable, often such notions are not terribly applicable. I sometimes joke that in doing Parts Work I am mostly just helping move furniture.

Further Topics

A handful of further topics helps fill out the book's observations and put them in larger perspective.

Parts Work and the Nature of the Self

Self-awareness is a popular topic in psychology, and we tend to take for granted what we mean by the phrase. But Parts Work suggests that, as often as not, our understanding is only partial. This limitation to our understanding is akin to the difference between Parts Work and humanistic approaches in psychotherapy. Culturally mature self-awareness is not just about looking within; it is about being able to hold in consciousness the entirety of one's complexity—the whole creative "box of crayons." We come back to how an appreciation of the Myth of the Individual gave being an individual a whole new meaning. In a similar way, Integrative Meta-perspective fundamentally alters what it means to have a Self.

Parts in Everyday Life

Not only do we tend to confuse identity with parts; we also often fail to notice how often we encounter parts in our daily lives. We've seen how all sorts of relationships historically have been of the two-halves-makes-whole kind. Whether the object of our perceptions is a leader, a lover, or a friend; most of the time—much more than we imagine—we are perceiving projected parts.

A good place to recognize the role that parts play in our perception of the world is the way we idealize prominent figures in popular media and find mythologized fascination in the minutia of their emotional lives. We see this parts-fueled fascination carried into stage plays and movies, where the conflict is usually between only certain aspects of characters' complexities rather than between whole people.

And as I hope I've made obvious from the previous examples, beliefs that we most vehemently cling to are usually not the conclusions of ourselves as whole people, but the beliefs of specific parts within us that have particular influence. One of the most powerful results of doing Parts Work is learning to be cautious about believing what we think.

Multiple Intelligences

A central notion in Creative Systems Theory is that intelligence is multiple. Besides our rationality, in which we take appropriate pride, human understanding also has emotional, imaginal, and bodily aspects. One of the benefits of Parts Work is that it makes intelligence's creative multiplicity explicit. When a person is first bringing parts into the room, I try to pay attention to what intelligences are being represented. If a major aspect of intelligence is missing, I can be pretty sure that later in the process a part will emerge that gives it voice; and often, that additional part will prove to be one of the most important.

Polarity and the Creative Nature of Truth

One of the most striking recognitions that emerges while doing Parts Work is how often parts juxtapose into polar relationships; more specifically they tend to polarize into archetypally masculine and archetypally feminine qualities. Imbedded in these recognitions is a basic observation about the nature of truth.

Creative Systems Theory (CST) proposes that we can never know ultimate truth. But what we can know is what appears to be true as a product of the way we understand. And CST describes how, in the end, intelligence is ordered creatively. We can see this by examining the structures of intelligence's multiplicity and by appreciating the underlying archetypally masculine and archetypally feminine symmetry between parts. We begin to see how human cognition is by its nature "pro-creative."

Thinking of that underlying symmetry in a more "bare-boned" way helps us recognize its manifestations in the history of understanding. Creative Systems Theory delineates how polarity juxtaposes unity/connectedness on one hand with separation/difference on the other.

We can recognize these observations in how I've spoken of different polar fallacies: unity fallacies, separation, and compromise fallacies. We can also derive essential insight into what makes something true. Notice how we see polarity reflected in our most basic notions about ultimate truth throughout history. For example, we find it with the polarity of spiritual versus material, which has historically divided understanding into religion on one hand and science on the other. We've seen how Parts Work challenges us to see "spiritual" and "material" only as parts. At this most basic of levels, it makes clear that truth—at least truth as we can know it—is ultimately "creative." The theory proposes that the recognition that human intelligence is creatively ordered provides a new Fundamental Organizing Concept for understanding—and truth—as a whole.

Our attempts to understand life provide an illustration of the importance of this kind of recognition. Modern Age thought provided two explanations: On one hand is mechanism, the theory that the physical world can be explained in purely mechanistic terms; while on the other hand is vitalism, the notion that some separate animating force, some inner essence, is also necessary. Most scientists today consider vitalism naive at best (appropriately). But we are left with the question of whether mechanism by itself can really get us there. Perhaps we might best think of each explanation as a part that is more a product of how we think, or at least how we have thought in times past, than what is actually the case.

Temperament and Parts Work

Creative Systems Theory describes how human intelligence is not merely "multiple," but that it is ordered "creatively." The Creative Systems Personality Typology[4] goes on to delineate that we can understand personality differences in terms of which aspects of intelligence's generative complexity that a person most draws on. Not surprisingly, we can see this in the characteristic that most stands out in a person's parts.

The primary personality constellations in the typology reflect native affinity with the sensibilities of one particular period in formative process—from generativity's germinal beginnings (Early-Axis temperaments), to the bringing of new possibility into manifest form (Middle-Axis temperaments), to a time of finishing and completion (Late-Axis temperaments). Within a business, for example, the "germinal" sensibilities stand out in the wild innovators and nerdy "eggheads" in research and development. We find more "manifest" sensibilities in engineers, managers, and hands-on workers who make sure new discoveries are practical, and then turn them into tangible products. And we find "finishing and polishing" sensibilities in the financial, design, and marketing types who take care of money matters, make products attractive to buyers, and make them widely available.

We can make several useful personality style generalities when it comes to doing Parts Work. First, people's parts will tend to have characteristics

---

[4] *The Creative Systems Personality Typology: Engaging the Generative Roots of Diversity,* by *Charles M. Johnston, MD, 2023, ICD Press 2023.*

consistent with their personality styles, although they are not always going to match their temperaments. Indeed, it is often through drawing on the creative diversity of one's parts that a person comes to grasp the power of culturally mature perspective. However, the parts that will most stand out will be consistent across people of the same temperament.

There are also differences in the ease with which people engage Parts Work. With some patients, Parts Work is effective no matter what their temperaments. But in general, Earlies tend to jump right in; Middles may take a bit longer to warm to the method although they often find it quickly providing insight; and Lates may need to persist for a while before they appreciate the depth at which the method can work.

Interestingly, we also find patterns in the number of parts that people of different personality styles tend to work with. Earlies, with their rich imaginations, often juggle numerous characters (sometimes as many as eight or ten) and find no problem keeping track of them all. Middles may pull off multiple characters in getting started, but will tend to settle on two or three. Lates are more likely to identify four or five characters and to engage in gradually deepening conversations with all of them over time.

Appendix B contains an expanded discussion of the Creative Systems Personality Typology. Complete coverage of the Typology is contained in my book, *The Creative Systems Personality Typology: Engaging the Generative Roots of Diversity*, 2023, ICD Press.

Parts Work and Psychopathology

Parts Work is generally not appropriate for people with severe psychopathology, although it can be valuable as a model for their therapist to keep in mind. But consciously separating parts can be disorganizing just when a person is most needing greater psychological organization.

Parts Work and the History of Belief

It is not unusual for someone on first encountering Parts Work to notice a similarity to an earlier culture when people paid homage to pantheons of gods—early Olympian Greece, classical Egypt, the Mesoamerican civilizations. The recognition that in times past we have thought of the most fundamental determiners of truth in terms of parts need not stop there. In the Middle Ages, we conceived of determination in terms of the warring influences God and the devil. And, while in modern times we like to think we have left the past's superstitions behind us, we have continued to think in terms of polarities, as evident in my earlier referrals to our juxtaposing of spiritual with material and vitalism with materialism, even in our modern age.

What can we learn from this recognition? Most immediately, it alerts us to the fact that we have always perceived our worlds through the language of parts. (Creative Systems Theory can explain the particular relationships between parts that we have established at various stages in the evolution of culture.)

It also highlights the major significance of Integrative Meta-perspective in the history of understanding. With culturally mature understanding, for the first time our understanding is not based on polarization and projection.

We must take care with this claim: It is not to say that for the first time we can understand objectively. In fact, Integrative Meta-perspective emphasizes that objectivity is not a possibility. (It makes clear that the only kind of understanding that is possible is through one's own intelligence.) And it brings attention to how objective versus subjective is itself a limiting polarity. In addition, it cautions against reaching conclusions that might seem to go beyond polarization but ultimately fail, such as siding with atheism over the claims of religious advocates.

What this recognition does do is affirm the observation—at a foundational level—that what we understand is a product of how we understand. And it highlights how Integrative Meta-perspective might make it possible to understand in ways that are more complete, more reflective of who we are as living, human beings.

AFTERWORD

We've seen how Parts Work has dramatic implications: It provides new insight into the practice of psychotherapy; it helps make understandable—and helps make manifest—essential cultural changes such as those currently reshaping our ideas of gender and identity; it offers a tool for getting beyond the discord and polarization that can make just getting along today difficult; it helps support the kind of leadership in all parts of our lives that times ahead will increasingly require; and it offers a way to address many big-picture questions that in times past might have left us baffled.

We are also pleasantly surprised that, in the hands of someone who is skilled with Parts Work, the process is remarkably straightforward, although applying it does require well-developed, culturally mature capacities on the part of the practitioner. But it doesn't demand a complex understanding of psychodynamics, unconscious processes, or cultural dynamics. For a person who is ready, it is not that hard to teach.

Hopefully you have found this brief emersion into the Parts Work methodology useful—and at least in some small way, enlightening.

APPENDIX A

Creative Systems Theory and the Concept of Cultural Maturity—An Introduction

Many readers will appreciate more of an introduction to Creative Systems Theory and the concept of Cultural Maturity. In the piece that follows, I provide additional background. I've touched briefly on many of its main observations in describing the basis for the typology. Think of these reflections as adding flesh to previous bare-boned conceptual observations. You can find a more extended introduction in the book *Insight: Creative Systems Theory's Radical New Picture of Human Possibility*.[5]

Background

Creative Systems Theory began in attempts to better understand the workings of creative processes. In time it evolved into an overarching framework for understanding purpose, change, and interrelationship in human systems. The theory has its foundation in the recognition that our meaning-making, toolmaking—we could say simply "creative"—nature is what ultimately defines us.

Creative Systems Theory concepts help us step back and appreciate culture's larger story; how human understanding has evolved over time. That includes not only the evolution of belief, but also the changing cognitive

---

[5] Charles M. Johnston, MD, *Insight: Creative Systems Theory's Radical New Picture of Creative Possibility*, 2022, ICD Press.

structures that have produced those beliefs. And specifically, it includes changes that reorder understanding in our time. The theory's comprehensive framework offers a way to replace Modern Age mechanistic thinking with ideas that better reflect that we are alive, and alive in the way that makes us human.

The concept of Cultural Maturity follows from Creative Systems Theory's larger picture. Much of my life's work has involved attempting to make sense of critical challenges ahead for the species. My focus had been less on technical challenges than on human challenges. Central to these efforts has been the observation that effectively addressing many of the most important of these challenges will require new kinds of human abilities. That observation shifted from an obstacle to something more consistent with hope, when I recognized that at least the potential for these new abilities was built into who we are. We don't have to invent them from whole cloth. The Creative Systems concept of Cultural Maturity describes the core task of our time as a new—and newly possible—"growing up" as a species.[6] Cultural Maturity involves changes not just in what we think, but how we think. These changes make essential new abilities possible. They also make possible new ways of thinking, such as Creative Systems Theory.

My efforts over the years have approached the ideas of Creative Systems Theory and the concept of Cultural Maturity from multiple directions. I've endeavored to clarify their essential roles in helping us address questions ahead in all parts of our lives—from the challenges of effective leadership and governance to what love and human relationships more generally will require of us. With my direction of the Institute for Creative Development (a Seattle-based think tank and center for advanced leadership training), I worked for

---

[6] I first introduced Creative Systems Theory and the concept of Cultural Maturity with my 1984 book *The Creative Imperative: Human Growth and Planetary Evolution* (Celestial Arts). The book *Creative Systems Theory: A Comprehensive Theory of Purpose, Change, and Interrelationship in Human Systems* (2021, ICD Press) provides the most detailed description of the theory.

twenty-five years to teach about and foster culturally mature leadership. And I've written over a dozen books and numerous articles that in various ways expand on the ideas of Creative Systems Theory and the broader implications of culturally mature understanding.

Here I will touch briefly on the shift in perspective that Creative Systems Theory represents. I will then turn more specifically to the concept of Cultural Maturity and examine some of the new human capacities Cultural Maturity's changes make possible. I will take a closer look at some of Creative Systems Theory's more detailed formulations. And, in concluding, I will give some particular attention to the implications of these notions for the tasks of future leadership and summarize the evidence that what I have described is correct.

The Power of a Creative Frame

The insight that makes Creative Systems Theory's more detailed formulations wholly new is the power of a creative frame. Thinking in creative terms provides a new Fundamental Organizing Concept able to take us beyond machine model notions of times past. In a related way, the application of a creative frame transcends past romantic and idealist objections to mechanistic notions. We can think of a creative frame as following directly from Cultural Maturity's cognitive reordering.

Creative Systems Theory includes three basic kinds of "patterning concepts" —notions that help us think about truth in ways that better reflect that we are living beings. Each kind of patterning concept has its foundation in a creative reframing of cognition. Patterning in Time concepts concern truth's temporal relativity. They address change processes in human systems—the dynamics of innovation, individual development, the growth of relationships, and, of particular importance, the evolution of culture. Patterning in Space notions address here-and-now contextual relativity. We can use them to help make sense of inner psychological dynamics as well as the workings of larger systems, from families and organizations to nations. The Creative Systems Personality Typology is the most fully developed Patterning in Space tool. The third group of notions, what the theory calls Whole-Person/Whole-System patterning concepts, address more general questions of possibility, motivation, and capacity.

Cultural Maturity

The Creative Systems Theory concept of Cultural Maturity focuses more specifically on today. It presents a new guiding narrative able to replace Modern Age assumptions that today, more and more, fail to serve us. It also describes new kinds of skills and capacities that will be needed if we are to effectively make our way. And it delineates how the task involves not just thinking new things, but thinking in new, more complete, and systemic ways. We can think of culturally mature perspective as providing the future's needed "new common sense." Creative Systems Theory's overarching formulations reflect this more mature and complete kind of perspective.

The concept of Cultural Maturity is not as easy a notion as the simple phrase "growing up" might suggest. For most people, it challenges our favorite assumptions. And it requires us to think in more encompassing ways than we are used to. But where it takes us is ultimately straightforward. I find it helpful to think of the changes that produce culturally mature understanding in a couple of steps. In the end, these steps reflect aspects of a single mechanism, but looking at them separately assists us in getting started.

The first change process gives the concept its name. Cultural Maturity brings a new, more mature relationship between culture and the individual. In times past, culture has functioned as a parent in the lives of individuals, providing us with clear rules to live by. These cultural absolutes worked to offer a sense of shared identity and connectedness with others. They also protected us from life's very real uncertainties and immense complexities.

Today, this traditional relationship is changing. Cultural absolutes are serving us less and less well. They are also having diminishing influence. This loss of past collective rules has Janus-faced implications. It can reveal possibilities that before now we could not have considered. But at the same time, it can bring a disturbing sense of absence. Clearly something more is needed. If all that we are seeing today is a loss of past parental guideposts, we have problems. The new possibility would be only of the postmodern, anything-goes, everybody-gets-their-own-truth, sort. What might seem to be freedom would produce instead only a loss of order and a dangerous kind of aimlessness.

The second kind of change process is what makes today's loss of past absolutes anything to celebrate. Cultural Maturity is not just about acting in more grown-up ways. It involves developmentally predicted cognitive changes. It turns out that the same change mechanisms that generate today's loss of past truths also create the potential for new, more mature ways of understanding. One way to think of culturally mature thought is that it is post-postmodern.

Creative Systems Theory uses an ungainly (but quite precise) term for the cognitive reordering that gives us Cultural Maturity and its new vantage for understanding: Integrative Meta-perspective. Integrative Meta-perspective involves, first, a more complete kind of stepping back from our complex natures. This stepping back creates greater awareness. It is also what creates new distance from culture's past parental role. And at the same time, Cultural Maturity's cognitive changes involve a new and deeper kind of engagement with the whole of our cognitive complexity, all the diverse aspects of who we are. The result is not just further abstraction, but the more fully embodied kind of understanding that is needed for mature decision-making.[7]

---

[7] My book *Rethinking How We Think: Integrative Meta-Perspective and the Cognitive "Growing Up" On Which Our Future Depends* (2020, ICD Press) provides a detailed examination of this cognitive reordering.

We will come back shortly for a closer look. For now, it is enough to appreciate that Integrative Meta-perspective, by allowing us to both more fully step back from and more deeply engage the whole of how we understand, lets us think in ways that are more encompassing and complete than was possible in times past. We could say that this new way of thinking is more systemic—or simply wiser. I often use the metaphor of a box of crayons. The crayons represent systemic aspects. The box represents a more encompassing perspective. Integrative Meta-perspective lets us step back and draw more consciously—and deeply—on the whole box.

New Questions and New Human Capacities

I've proposed that addressing critical questions before us will require new kinds of human capacities. One of the best arguments for the concept of Cultural Maturity is that its cognitive changes make needed new capacities possible. Noting a few of these capacities helps affirm the importance of Culturally Maturity's changes and highlights important aspects of where they take us.

Accepting a newly ultimate kind of responsibility: As we leave behind thinking of culture as a symbolic parent, we necessarily assume a new depth of responsibility, and not just for our actions, but for the truths we draw on.

Getting beyond the us-and-them polar assumptions of times past: The importance of this further capacity is most obvious with how it helps us begin to leave behind the "chosen people/evil other" polarizations that through history have led to war. Creative Systems Theory describes how relationships of all sorts—from those between nations, to those that define leadership, to those we find with friendship or love—have always before been based on projection. We've related not as whole beings, but as symbolic halves that together made a whole. The theory also describes how Integrative Meta-perspective's more systemic vantage helps us re-own the projections that before had produced mythologized perceptions of both the demonized and idealized sort. With Cultural Maturity's cognitive reordering, we become better able to act in the world as whole systems, and to engage other systems as whole systems.

Better appreciating the fact of limits: The Modern Age story was heroic: We celebrated a world without limits. Increasingly, however, we recognize that if we are not more attentive to real limits, we are doomed. Integrative Meta-perspective's more encompassing vantage makes clear that, whatever our concern, in the end limits come with the territory. The greater maturity that comes with Integrative Meta-perspective applies to real limits of every sort—limits to what we can do (as with environmental limits), limits to what we can know and predict (as we recognize with good risk assessment), and limits to what we can be for one another (as with culturally mature relationships of all sorts). It also reveals how a mature acknowledgement of limits, rather than limiting us, in the end increases possibility.

Learning to better tolerate complexity and uncertainty: Today, questions of every kind confront us with new complexities and uncertainties. Because Integrative Meta-perspective draws directly on our own systemic complexity, it helps us make sense of and tolerate complexity in the world around us. And for a related reason, Cultural Maturity's changes make us more comfortable in uncertainty's presence. Creative Systems Theory describes how ideas become ideological—and thus expressions of last-word truth—when we make one aspect of a larger complexity (one crayon in that systemic box) the whole of understanding. When we engage in understanding more fully, uncertainty becomes intrinsic to any deep understanding of truth. Creative Systems Theory goes further to describe how both complexity and uncertainty are necessary ingredients in cognition's "creative" workings.

Learning to think about what matters in more systemically complete ways: With Integrative Meta-perspective we become able to "measure" significance in ways that better reflect the whole of who we are and the whole of anything we might wish to consider. For example, moral decisions become less about choosing between good and evil than about acknowledging competing goods and discerning where the most life-affirming choices ultimately lie. And as relationships of all sorts require us to step beyond two-halves-make-a-whole projective dynamics, in a similar way, Integrative Meta-perspective lets us more directly discern when a human connection enhances life. This new capacity applies most broadly to the critical task of rethinking advancement. Our times demand that we think about wealth and progress in ways that are more encompassing and complete.

Better understanding how events happen in a context, particularly in the context of our time in culture's story: Thinking that serves us going forward must help us make more dynamic and nuanced kinds of discernments. Of particular importance, it must help us be more attentive to context. With culturally mature truth, the "when" and the "where" are always as important as the "what." Such contextual relativity is wholly different from relativity of the postmodern, anything-goes sort. Culturally mature understanding allows us to make highly precise distinctions that are precise exactly because they take contextual nuances into account. We can think of Creative Systems Theory's framework for understanding purpose, change, and interrelationship in human systems as a set of tools for making such context-specific observations. The Creative Systems Personality Typology[8] is a specific example of this kind of contribution.

Integrative Meta-perspective and Polarity

A closer look at the cognitive reorganization that underlies Cultural

---

[8] The Creative Systems Personality Typology: Engaging the Generative Roots of Diversity, by Charles M. Johnston, MD, 2023, ICD Press 2023.

Maturity's changes helps us appreciate why such new capacities result, and ties them more directly to Creative Systems Theory's conceptual framework. I've described how Integrative Meta-perspective involves at once more fully stepping back from and more deeply engaging the whole of our human complexity. Reflecting briefly on a couple of ways of thinking about that complexity—the role of polarity in how we think and the fact of intelligence's multiplicity—provides important further insight.

Let's first consider the fact of polarity. Creative Systems Theory describes how each chapter in culture's story to this point has framed truth in terms of qualities set in polar juxtaposition (for example, in modern times, mind versus body, leader versus follower, or science versus religion). Robert Frost observed that "It almost scares a man the way things come in pairs." With Cultural Maturity's cognitive reordering, we both step back from and more deeply engage past either/or relationships. In the process, we become able to appreciate them as aspects of larger systemic realities.

Creative Systems Theory brings detail to what we see. As a start, it addresses why we see polarity in the first place. After proposing that what most makes us human is our meaning-making, toolmaking, "creative" prowess, it goes on to describe how our cognitive mechanisms are designed to support this capacity for innovation. Specifically, regarding polarity, it describes how the fact that we think in polar terms follows directly from this creative picture.

Creative Systems Theory delineates how the same progression of polar relationships orders creative/formative change of all sorts—from an act of invention to the evolution of culture. Such change begins with a newly created aspect budding off from its original context. With each succeeding stage in formative process's first half, polar aspects become more separate, juxtaposing in evolving, creatively predicted ways. With the second, more mature half of any formative process, polarities reconcile to create a new and larger whole. We come to experience the newly created entity now as "second nature."

This sequence provides a template for understanding formative processes wherever we might find it. Creative Systems Theory calls the generic map that results—applicable to formative dynamics from the most personal of insights to the most encompassing of collective processes—the Creative Function.

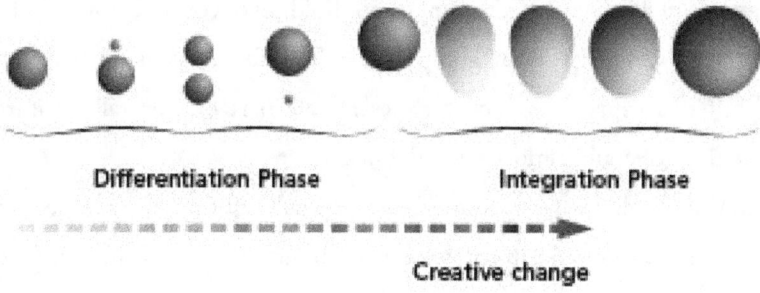

Fig. A-1: The Creative Function

We can recognize this two-part extended picture in personal psychological development. The underlying impetus with development in the first half of an individual life is toward distinction and the establishing of identity as form. With childhood we begin discovering who we are, with adolescence we make our first forays into the social world, and during adulthood we establish our unique place in that world. Second-half-of-life maturing involves more specifically integrative tasks: It is about learning how to live in the world with the greatest perspective, depth, and integrity.

When applied at a cultural scale, this picture of evolving polar relationships has critical implications for understanding the times in which we live. I've described Cultural Maturity's "growing up" in how we think and act in terms of Integrative Meta-perspective and the more encompassing kind of understanding it makes possible. Integrative Meta-perspective helps us get our minds around apparent polar opposites on the largest of scales. The Creative Function helps us appreciate how Cultural Maturity's cognitive reordering is a predicted consequence of our time in culture's evolving creative story.

We don't need Creative Systems Theory's detailed formulations to appreciate the relationship between polarity and Integrative Meta-perspective. F. Scott Fitzgerald proposed that the sign of a first-rate intelligence (we might say a mature intelligence) is the ability to hold two contradictory truths simultaneously in mind without going mad. His reference was to personal maturity, but this capacity is such an inescapable part of culturally mature perspective that we could almost say it defines it.

One of the simplest ways to think about how culturally mature perspective changes the way we understand draws on the basic observation that needed new understandings of every sort "bridge" polar assumptions of times past.[9] We can think of Cultural Maturity's point of departure as itself a "bridging" dynamic. We step back and see the relationship of culture and the individual in more encompassing terms. Cultural Maturity "bridges" ourselves and our societal contexts (or, put another way, ourselves and final truth). It is through this most fundamental "bridging" that we leave behind society's past parental function.

This most encompassing linkage holds within it a multitude of more local "bridging." Nothing more characterized the last century's defining conceptual advances than their linking of previously unquestioned polar truths. Physics' new picture provocatively circumscribed the realities of matter and energy, space and time, object and observer. New understandings in biology more closely linked humankind with the natural world, and by reopening timeless questions about life's origins, joined the purely physical with the organic. And

---

[9] I organized my early book *Necessary Wisdom: Meeting the Challenge of a New Cultural Maturity* (1991, Celestial Arts) around this basic observation.

the ideas of modern psychology, neurology, and sociology have provided an increasingly integrated picture of the workings of conscious with unconscious, mind with body, self with society, and more.

If the relationship between "bridging" and Cultural Maturity is to make ultimately useful sense, we need to include a couple of critical distinctions. We need first to clearly distinguish between personal maturity and Cultural Maturity. The ability to hold contradictory truths that F. Scott Fitzgerald described has been a characteristic of wise thought throughout history. In contrast, none of the last century's defining insights that I just noted would have made sense before now. The "bridging" of cultural realities that the concept of Cultural Maturity describes is specifically a phenomenon of our time.

We must also avoid confusing "bridging" as I am using the term with more familiar outcomes (which is why I put the word in quotes). The result is wholly different from averaging or compromise, from walking the white line in the middle of the road. And just as fundamentally it is different from simple oneness, the collapsing of one pole into the other that we commonly see with more spiritual interpretations. "Bridging" in this sense is about consciously drawing on the whole creative box of crayons.

Cultural Maturity and Intelligence's Creative Multiplicity

Framing Cultural Maturity's cognitive reordering in terms of intelligence's multiplicity provides further nuance and helps us better put the changes that result—and their significance—in historical perspective. Creative Systems Theory highlights how intelligence has multiple parts. Besides our rationality (in which we take appropriate pride), intelligence has other aspects, some more emotional or symbolic, others more sensory.

Most of what Creative Systems Theory has to say about our diverse ways of knowing is beyond the scope of this appendix,[10] but certain observations are specifically relevant. Especially pertinent is how Creative Systems Theory explains why we have multiple intelligences. The theory delineates how our various intelligences work together to support and drive our creative proclivities. We find a related intelligence-specific progression with every kind of human formative process—be it invention, individual development, the growth of a relationship, or, of particular importance for these reflections, the evolution of culture. Different aspects of intelligence and different relationships between intelligences most define experience at different creative stages.

Creative Systems Theory delineates four basic types of intelligence. For ease of conversation, we can refer to them simply as the intelligences of the body, the imagination, the emotions, and the intellect. (The theory uses the fancier language that I include in Figure A-2.) CST proposes that these different ways of knowing represent more than merely diverse approaches to processing information. They represent the windows through which we make sense of our worlds and the formative tendencies that lead us to shape our worlds in the ways that we do.

This observation has major practical implications. It provides the basis for Creative Systems Theory's framework for understanding the workings of human systems. It also has consequences of a more philosophical and paradigmatic sort. I've hinted at how Creative Systems Theory is significant not only because it provides new conceptual tools for making our way, but also because it successfully takes us beyond the kind of thinking that has defined Modern Age understanding.

---

[10] For the broader discussion see Charles M. Johnston, MD, *Intelligence's Creative Multiplicity: And Its Critical Role in the Future of Understanding*, 2023, ICD Press.

PARTS WORK

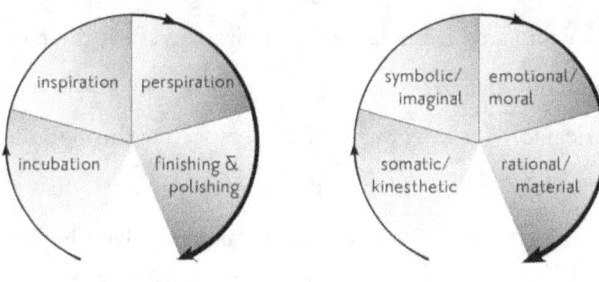

The Stages of Formative Process

Multiple Intelligences

Fig. A-2: Formative Process and Intelligence's Creative Multiplicity

This observation has major practical implications. It provides the basis for Creative Systems Theory's framework for understanding the workings of human systems. It also has consequences of a more philosophical and paradigmatic sort. I've hinted at how Creative Systems Theory is significant not only because it provides new conceptual tools for making our way, but also because it successfully takes us beyond the kind of thinking that has defined Modern Age understanding.

Enlightenment thinkers such as Sir Isaac Newton and René Descartes described reality as a great clockwork. While machine-model thinking has made a huge contribution—it has given us not only scientific and industrial advancement, but our modern concept of the individual, as well—it presents real problems if we wish to talk about living systems. There is no more significant conceptual challenge in our time than finding ways to address human systems more directly in living terms. Any culturally mature notion at least implies this important conceptual leap, but Creative Systems Theory makes it explicit. I've proposed that the creative frame which serves as the theory's foundation represents a new Fundamental Organizing Concept that effectively takes us beyond the mechanistic assumptions of times past. By drawing on this dynamic and generative approach to understanding, the theory can provide highly delineated formulations that directly reflect the fact that we are living—and human—beings.

A more historical look at Integrative Meta-perspective through the lens of intelligence's multiplicity helps fill out the conceptual leap that produces culturally mature understanding. Modern Age thought similarly had its origins in a new kind of cognitive orientation. And stepping back from previous ways of knowing was a big part of it. We became better able to step back from the more mystical sensibilities that gave us the beliefs of the Middle Ages.

Along with this more general stepping back, rationality came to have a newly central significance. The rational now stood clearly separate from the subjective aspects of experience and became specifically allied with conscious awareness. The result was a new, as-if-from-a-balcony sense of clarity and objectivity. This, combined with the new belief in the individual as a logical choice-maker that accompanied it, produced all the great advances of the Modern Age.

But while Modern Age thought was a grand achievement, Integrative Meta-perspective's stepping back represents a wholly different sort of accomplishment. Awareness comes to stand more fully separate from the whole of our intelligence's systemic complexity—including the rational. Integrative Meta-perspective offers that we might step back equally from aspects of ourselves that we formerly treated as objective and those that we had thought of as subjective. In the process, it offers that we might better step back from the whole of intelligence.

And there is more. Culturally mature understanding requires not only that we be aware of intelligence's multiple aspects, but also that in a whole new sense we embody each of these aspects. It directly draws on all of our diverse ways of knowing. Culturally mature understanding requires thinking in a rational sense—indeed, it expands rationality's role. But just as much it involves more directly plumbing the feeling, imagining, and sensing aspects of who we are. And this is the case as much for the most rigorous of hard theory as when our concerns are more personal. Making sense of most anything about us—the values we hold, the nature of identity, what it means to have human relationships—increasingly requires this more encompassing kind of understanding.

An important outcome when we frame Cultural Maturity in this way might at first seem contradictory. On one hand, because culturally mature perspective draws on multiple, often conflicting aspects of who we are, its conclusions are less absolute and once-and-for-all than those we are used to. I've described how they require that we be more comfortable with complexity and uncertainty. But, at the same time, we can appropriately argue that culturally mature understanding is more "objective" than what it replaces. Certainly it is more complete.

Enlightenment thought might have claimed ultimate objectivity, but this was in fact objectivity of only a limited sort. Besides leaving culture's parental status untouched, it left experience as a whole divided—objective (in the old sense) set opposed to subjective, mind set opposed to body, thoughts set opposed to feelings (and anything else that does not conform to modernity's rationalist/materialist worldview). We cannot ultimately claim to be objective if we have left out half of the evidence. Culturally mature objectivity is of a more specifically all-the-crayons-in-the-box sort.

The fact that we can understand Cultural Maturity in terms of developmentally predicted cognitive changes also points toward an important further implication suggested earlier. It supports being legitimately optimistic about what may lie ahead. If Cultural Maturity's cognitive changes are, as potential built into who we are, the likelihood that we can thrive and prosper in times ahead increases significantly. And, if this is a cognitive reordering that we can actively practice and facilitate, that likelihood increases further.[11]

Creative Systems Theory and the Application of a Creative Frame

We can arrive at a creative frame in multiple ways. As a start, we can do so by reflecting on what Integrative Meta-perspective teaches us about the workings of polarity. And we don't need the Creative Functions developmental picture to get there. I've described how culturally mature understanding "bridges" the polarized assumptions of times past. If we look closely, we recognize that polar relationships reflect an underlying symmetry. I've noted how polarities juxtapose some softer, we could say, more left hand—or to use language from psychology, more archetypally feminine—quality, with another quality that is harder, we could say, more right-hand—or more archetypally masculine. Creative Systems Theory describes how this basic symmetry is key to the workings of formative process. I've emphasized the important sense in which the relationship between the two hands of any polarity when understood systemically becomes "procreative."

We get to a similar place if we shift our attention to intelligence. I've described how Integrative Meta-perspective makes it possible to better hold the whole of human intelligence. And I've observed Creative Systems Theory's claim that intelligence's multiplicity functions to support and drive formative process. Integrative Meta-perspective, just from where it takes us, thrusts us into a world in which the workings of intelligence are dynamic and systemic, and this in a whole new sense—we could say in a sense that is expressly creative.

A closer look at intelligence's multiplicity and its role in formative process helps fill out this creative picture. It also provides a glimpse into how Creative

---

11 See Charles M Johnston, MD, *Hope and the Future: Confronting Today's Crisis of Purpose*, 2018, ICD Press.

Systems Patterning in Time notions help us understand change in human systems. Creative Systems Theory proposes that we are the uniquely creative creatures we are, not merely because we are conscious, but because of the ways that the various aspects of our intelligence work, and how they work together. The theory describes how our various intelligences—or we might better say, "sensibilities" to reflect all that they encompass—relate in specifically creative ways. And it delineates how different ways of knowing, and different relationships between ways of knowing, predominate at specific times in any human change processes. The way Creative Systems Theory ties the underlying structures of intelligence to patterns of change in human systems both helps us better understand change and hints at the possibility of better predicting it.

The theory argues that our various intelligences work together in ways that are not merely collaborative, but specifically creative. It describes how human intelligence is uniquely configured to support creative change—to drive and facilitate its workings. Our various modes of intelligence, juxtaposed like colors on a color wheel, function together as creativity's mechanism. That wheel, like the wheel of a car or a Ferris wheel, is continually turning, continually in motion. The way the various facets of intelligence juxtapose makes change, and specifically purposeful change, inherent to our natures.

With creativity's initial "incubation" stage, the dominant intelligence is the kinesthetic, body intelligence, if you will. It is like I am pregnant, but don't yet know quite with what. What I do know takes the form of "inklings" and faint "glimmerings," inner sensing. If I want to feed this part of the creative process, I do things that help me to be reflective and to connect in my body. I take a long walk in the woods, draw a warm bath, build a fire in the fireplace.

Next comes creativity's "inspiration" stage, the stage in which new possibility first comes into the light. The dominant intelligence here is the imaginal—that which most defines art, myth, and the let's-pretend world of young children. The products of this period in the creative process may appear suddenly—Archimedes's "Eureka"—or they may come more subtly and gradually. It is this stage, and this part of our larger sensibility, that we tend to most traditionally associate with things creative.

With creativity's "perspiration" stage we give inspiration solid form. The dominant intelligence is different still, more emotional and visceral—the intelligence of heart and guts. It is here that we confront the hard work of finding the right approach and the most satisfying means of expression. We also confront limits to our skills and are challenged to push beyond them. The perspiration stage tends to bring a new moral commitment and emotional edginess. We must compassionately but unswervingly confront what we have created if it is to stand the test of time.

With creativity's "finishing and polishing" stage we give creation detail and engage the tasks of completion. Here, rational intelligence comes to have the more dominant role. This period is more conscious and more concerned with aesthetic precision than the periods previous. It is also more concerned with audience and outcome. It brings final focus to the creative work, the clarity of thought and nuances of style needed for effective communication.

While we might assume that the creative task is now done, we've in fact come at best half of the way. And the changes that mark formative process's second half are equally as important and transforming. With creation's second half, we step back from the work and appreciate it with a new perspective. We become more able to appreciate the relationship of the work to its creative contexts: both ourselves and the time and place in which it was created. The result of this "seasoning" process is a more integrative picture. I've spoken of how the work becomes in a new sense, "second nature." Specifically, regarding intelligence, we come to use our diverse ways of knowing more consciously together. We become better able to apply our intelligences in various combinations and balances as time and situation warrant and through this process to engage the work as a whole and ourselves in relationship to it.

We can tie this progression to formative processes of all sorts. We see something similar whether our concern is an act of innovation, personal psychological development, or culture and its evolution. For example, we find the same bodily intelligence that orders creative "incubation" playing a particularly prominent role in the infant's rhythmic world of movement, touch, and taste. The realities of early tribal cultures also draw deeply on body sensibilities. Truth in tribal societies is synonymous with the rhythms of nature and, through dance, song, story, and drumbeat, with the body of the tribe.

We find the same imaginal intelligence that we saw ordering creative "inspiration" taking prominence in the play-centered world of the young child. We also hear it voiced with strength in early civilizations—such as ancient Greece or Egypt, the Incas and Aztecs in the Americas, or the classical East—with their mythic pantheons and great symbolic tales.

We find the same emotional and moral intelligence that orders creative "perspiration" occupying center stage in adolescence, with its deepening passions and pivotal struggles for identity. It can also be felt with strength in the beliefs and values of the European Middle Ages, times marked by feudal struggle and ardent moral conviction (and, today, where struggle and conflict seem to be forever recurring).

In a similar way, we find the same rational intelligence that comes forward for the "finishing and polishing" tasks of creativity taking new prominence in young adulthood, as we strive to create our unique place in the world of adult expectations. This more refined and refining aspect of intelligence stepped to the fore culturally during the Renaissance and the Age of Reason and, in the West, has held sway in modern times.

Finally, and of pertinence to the concept of Cultural Maturity, we find the same, more consciously integrative relationship to intelligence that we see in the "seasoning" stage of a creative act ordering the unique developmental capacities—the wisdom—of a lifetime's second half. We can also see this same, more integrative relationship with intelligence just beneath the surface in our current cultural stage in the Western advances that have transformed understanding through the last century.

We associate the Age of Reason with Descartes's assertion that "I think, therefore I am." We could make a parallel assertion for each of these other cultural stages: "I am embodied, therefore I am"; "I imagine, therefore I am"; "I am a moral being, therefore I am"; and, if the concept of Cultural Maturity is accurate, "I understand maturely and systemically—with the whole of myself—therefore I am." The concept of Cultural Maturity proposes that the words you have just read about intelligence's creative workings have made sense because such consciously integrative dynamics are beginning to reorder how we think and perceive.

Creative Systems Theory Patterning Concepts

I've observed how Creative Systems Theory includes three basic kinds of "patterning concepts." Patterning in Time concepts address change in human systems. The chart in Figure A-3 summarizes Creative Systems Theory Patterning in Time observations as they pertain to common developmental processes—a simple creative act, individual human development, the growth of a relationship, and, of particular importance, the history of culture. It also adds the language that the theory uses in making such distinctions: Pre-Axis for "incubation stage" sensibilities, Early-Axis for "inspiration stage" sensibilities, Middle-Axis for "perspiration stage" sensibilities, and Late-Axis for "finishing and polishing" stage sensibilities.

			CREATIVE STAGES			
Pre-Axis	Early-Axis	Middle-Axis	Late-Axis	Transition		Integrative Stages
			MAJOR PERIODICITIES			
A CREATIVE EVENT						
Incubation	Inspiration	Perspiration	Finishing & Polishing	Presentation		Becoming "Second Nature" (Integration of the newly created form into self and culture)
A LIFETIME						
Prenatal Period & Infancy	Childhood	Adolescence	Early Adulthood	Midlife Transition		Mature Adulthood (From knowledge to wisdom—integration of self as formed identity with the ground of being)
A RELATIONSHIP						
Pre-relationship	Falling in Love	Time of Struggle	Established Relationship	Time of Questioning		Mature Intimacy (Relationship as two whole people—marriage of the "loved" and the "lover" within each person)
THE HISTORY OF CULTURE						
Pre-History	Golden Ages	Middle Ages	Age of Reason	Transitional Culture		Cultural Maturity (Larger meeting of the form and context of culture)

Fig. A-3: Formative Process from the Perspective of Creative Systems Theory

Patterning in Space notions address here-and-now systemic differences. The Creative Systems Personality Typology is the most filled out and recognized Patterning in Space tool. But we can also use Patterning in Space notions to help tease apart internal psychological mechanisms and to map the dynamics and interactions of interpersonal relationships, organizations, communities, nations, and the planet as a whole.

The third kind of patterning notions, what the theory calls Whole-Person/Whole-System patterning concepts, address attributes that are products of systems as entireties. They address what truth at its most basic becomes with Culture Maturity's cognitive reordering. Some examples include the concept of Aliveness, a general way of talking about possibility and motivation; the idea of Capacitance, a measure of overall human capacity; and the notion of Creative Symptoms, a way of thinking about protective mechanisms in human systems.

Creative Systems Theory Patterning concepts provide overarching perspective for understanding what makes us who we are and what good choices look like in today's world. They offer a comprehensive set of tools—applicable to both individuals and social systems—for making our way in a culturally mature reality.

The Dilemma of Trajectory and Transitional Absurdity

A couple of further Creative Systems concepts are important to touch on briefly if what we see in our times is to make full sense. The first, what Creative Systems Theory calls the Dilemma of Trajectory, describes how Cultural Maturity's changes involve more than just letting go of one cultural stage and moving to another, how they bring into question the whole developmental orientation that has previously defined growth and truth. The Dilemma of Trajectory makes changes at least like those that the concept of Cultural Maturity describes inescapably necessary.

We can describe the Dilemma of Trajectory in multiple ways. Most simply, we can frame it using the language of polarity. Creative Systems Theory delineates how each stage in culture to this point has been defined by greater distinction between polar opposites and a greater general emphasis on difference. (In tribal times, connectedness to nature and tribe was primary; today materiality and individuality prevails.) We can also frame the Dilemma of Trajectory in terms of intelligence's multiplicity. We've evolved from times in which the more creatively germinal aspects of intelligence—the body and the imagination—most informed experience (to be part of a tribe is to know the tribal dances and rituals) to times in which the rational—with a limited contribution from the emotional—holds the much larger influence (enter the Age of Reason). We can also describe this evolution in terms of culture's story—how it has taken us from times in which archetypally feminine influences ruled to times in which the archetypally masculine is the defining presence.

In our time, this organizing trajectory has reached an extreme: Truth has come to be defined almost exclusively by difference (for example, we view objective and subjective as wholly separate worlds); we equate rationality with understanding; and extreme archetypally masculine values prevail (such as those of the marketplace and science). The Dilemma of Trajectory alerts us to the danger of going further in this direction. Indeed, in an important sense, it stops being an option. We would not do well if we lost what remaining connection we have with nature, or bodies, or the more receptive aspects of experience that form the basis of human relationships. Continuing our current trajectory would irretrievably alienate us from aspects of who we are that are essential to being human.

So what are we to do? We could go back—a proposal at least implied in certain kinds of social advocacy. But going back is not any more likely to get us where we need to go. Unless there is a further option, the human experiment could be at an end. By reconciling the Dilemma of Trajectory, Integrative Meta-perspective offers a possible way forward. And it is a way forward that points toward an essential kind of human realization and fulfillment.

The second additional concept relates to an observation that could seem to prove the concept of Cultural Maturity wrong. A lot that we see in today's world appears to be almost the opposite of what the concept predicts—for example, increasing political and social polarization, widespread denial regarding essential limits-related challenges such as climate change and the extinction of species, and the growing prevalence of authoritarian rule in places where we might have assumed it to be something of the past. Given that we find so much in contemporary human behavior that can seem ludicrous—and often rather scary—it can be hard to believe that getting wiser as a species is a possibility.

It may not be. But it turns out that much of what we see is consistent with the concept of Cultural Maturity. The concept predicts that our times should be characterized not just by new possibilities, but also by times of regression and distorted ways of thinking. Creative Systems Theory calls this kind of ludicrousness Transitional Absurdity.[12]

New Capacities and Critical Challenges

Creative Systems Theory argues that we will be able to address challenges ahead for the species—and in the process address the Dilemma of Trajectory and confront Transitional Absurdity—only to the degree we can begin to apply the new human capacities that I've described following from Cultural Maturity's cognitive reordering. Noting a few of those challenges and what they will ask of us helps clarify how this is so. Regarding better understanding personality style differences, in each case the more complete kind of self-awareness and the greater capacity for collaboration that comes with such understanding provides support for needed changes.

How can we act morally in a world without obvious moral guideposts? Until very recently, culture in its parental role has provided us with clear moral rules. Our task has been simply to understand and obey those rules. Today, traditional moral guideposts are losing their authority and the moral relativisms that tend to replace them leave us feeling rudderless. We find ourselves in an increasingly complex, change-permeated moral landscape. Cultural Maturity's cognitive changes offer that we might address moral questions with a new systemic depth and nuance—and, with it, a comfort with uncertainty and

---

12   I wrote the short book Perspective and Guidance for a Time of Deep Discord: Why We See Such Extreme Social and Political Polarization—and What We Can Do About It (2021, ICD Press) in response to some of today's particularly concerning Transitional Absurdities. Later, I wrote Transitional Absurdity: A Reason for Hope / A Reason to Fear—Looking Squarely at the Future in Confusing and Contradictory Times (2023, ICD Press), to further examine how to make sense of and survive the existential challenges we face today.

complexity that has not before been an option.

How do we keep from destroying ourselves? I've noted how collective identity through history has depended on dividing our worlds into "chosen people" and "evil others." This way of defining who we are is becoming increasingly problematic, with the nuclear genie now out of the bottle, and terrorism an inescapable threat. Our safety in the long term will depend on bringing greater maturity and sophistication to how we understand our human differences and how we relate to conflict. Integrative Meta-Perspective's systemically encompassing vantage offers the possibility of getting beyond the polarized and polarizing assumptions that have created us-versus-them worlds.

How do we avoid making the planet unlivable? Climate change, global industrialization, and the broader effects of growing human population threaten to make existence on the planet less and less pleasant. It is quite possible that the earth will eventually become unlivable even for us. If we are going to avoid such an outcome, we must step beyond our modern heroic mythology that views limits only as constraints to be overcome. Culturally mature perspective highlights the inherent role of limits in the workings of living systems and helps us engage them in the most creative ways.

In times ahead, how will the requirements of effective leadership change? Today, trust in leadership of all sorts is less than it was at the height of anti-authoritarian rhetoric in the 1960s. We could easily assume—and people have argued—that this modern lack of confidence in leadership reflects something gone terribly wrong—broad failure on the part of leaders, a loss of moral integrity on the part of those being led, or even an impending collapse of society. But if it does, there is little reason to have hope.

The concept of Cultural Maturity offers an explanation that is more optimistic, but also more demanding. It alerts us to the fact that the meaning of leadership is changing—and in all parts of our lives, from the leadership in ourselves needed to make good personal choices, to what is required to effectively lead organizations and nations. Along with altering how we go about making decisions, these changes invite important reflection about possible next chapters in the way we think about governance and how we structure our governmental institutions.

Leadership's new picture is not all positive. Today we reside in an awkward in-between time with these changes. When we do see leadership that begins to reflect culturally mature capacities, people are as likely to attack it as celebrate it. But if the concept of Cultural Maturity is correct, moving forward in how we embody and relate to leadership is both possible and essential.

How will love change in times ahead? Love might seem more a personal concern, less pertinent to big-picture cultural well-being. But certainly, the topic is relevant to people's sense of fulfillment. Changes we see today with love are also directly pertinent to what relationships of every kind will require of us in times ahead. Romantic love of the sort symbolized by Romeo and Juliet represented a powerful step forward from what came before it—marriages arranged by one's family or a matchmaker. But it can't be the last chapter in love's story. While we idealize such love as based on individual choice, it was never quite this. Modern romantic love makes the other person our completion—our white knight or fair maiden. Rather than love between whole people, what we have known is "two-halves-make-a-whole" love. Love today challenges us to love as whole beings. Integrative Meta-perspective makes such more Whole-Person love newly possible.[13] A related kind of change is reordering relationships of every sort. In the end, these changes challenge us to rethink not just relationships, but the nature of individual identity—and with this, what it means to choose and to live purposefully.

What will it mean to use technologies wisely in times ahead? Technological

---

[13] I examine this is a topic in depth in my book *On the Evolution of Intimacy: A Brief Exploration Into the Past, Present, and Future of Gender and Love* (2019, ICD Press).

innovations will be key to future advancement. But it is just as important if we are to have a healthy and survivable future that more effectively assesses their benefits and identifies potential unintended consequences. These might seem like wholly technical tasks. But, in fact, carrying them out with the needed sophistication will require a maturity of perspective that we have not before been capable of. It has been our Modern Age tendency to treat technology as a god. If we continue to do so, our profound capacities as tool makers could eventually be our undoing. Culturally mature perspective helps us get beyond technological gospel thinking and bring the nuance of understanding needed to apply new technologies wisely.

How must we define progress if our actions are to successfully take us forward? In modern times, we have thought of progress as an onward-and-upward trajectory of increasing individuality and material achievement. While this definition has served us well, it cannot continue to do so going forward, for multiple reasons. Beyond the fact that it is not environmentally sustainable, it should prove less and less successful at giving our lives purpose. Compelling pictures of advancement must consider the full measure of human needs—not just individual accomplishment and material accumulation, but also human relationships, creativity, the health of our bodies, our larger sense of connectedness in life, and much more.

There is a further critical reason why progress's past definition cannot continue to serve us, which I have just touched on. The Dilemma of Trajectory describes how continuing on as we have would sever us from aspects of who we are that are critical to being human. If this conclusion is accurate, it is not just that clinging to progress's familiar definition would be unwise: Doing so has stopped being an option. Our future depends on defining progress in more systemically complete ways.

As these multiple challenges make clear, like it or not we live in times that ask a lot of us. The important recognition is that, whatever the origins of today's increasingly demanding challenges, with sufficient courage and persistence Cultural Maturity works as an antidote.

Looking at the Evidence

Radical notions like Creative Systems Theory's application of a creative frame and the concept of Cultural Maturity require strong evidence. Here we've seen how Creative Systems Theory's developmental framework—whether we approach it through the lens of polarity or through the evolution of intelligence—provides valuable conceptual perspective. We've also looked at how the fact that Cultural Maturity's changes make needed new capacities possible supports the conclusion that something like what the concept describes will at least be necessary. In addition, we've seen how more specific notions like the Dilemma of Trajectory and Transitional Absurdity are consistent with what a creative frame predicts and makes the need for something at least similar to what the concept of Cultural Maturity describes impossible to escape.

There are other kinds of evidence for the power of a creative frame. For example, in my overarching book, *Creative Systems Theory*, I describe how its application lets us answer questions that have always left us baffled, indeed many quandaries of the "eternal" sort. It turns out that we need Integrative Meta-perspective not just to answer such questions, but to ask them in helpful ways. Some examples that I touch on in the book: How do we reconcile the experience of free will with what logically seems a deterministic world? Are the beliefs of science and religion merely different, or do they represent parts of a larger picture? And how do we best understand the human species 'place in the larger scheme of things?

More specifically regarding the concept of Cultural Maturity, for me the most compelling evidence that its thesis is correct is the simplest. I don't see another way of framing the human task that is consistent with a healthy and vital future. Indeed, I don't see another way of framing the human task that is ultimately survivable. If I have not missed something important, Cultural Maturity becomes the only option going forward, the only game in town.

An observation implied in Creative Systems Theory's developmental picture provides further support for Cultural Maturity's significance if it is correct. Cultural Maturity's changes may do more than provide an effective response to today's immediate challenges. They may offer a basic blueprint for the right thought and action applicable far into humanity's future. We can think of them as ultimate human achievement.

APPENDIX B

Creative Context and Intelligence's Multiplicity

In Chapter Six, I emphasized the importance of context in my discussions of temperament and the history of belief. One of the most striking recognitions when we step into Cultural Maturity's new territory of experience is how dramatically truth becomes contextual. When we leave behind history's shared parental absolutes and a time's more particular ideological beliefs, we are confronted by the fact that what matters depends on when and where we look. At first, such contextual relativity can be difficult to grasp. We are more used to thinking of significance as once-and-for-all and absolute. Or, if we do acknowledge the role of context, we are likely to stop with postmodern, anything-goes assumptions. One of the most important consequences of Cultural Maturity's cognitive reordering is that it allows us to make highly precise discernments that are precise precisely because they take contextual nuance into account.

We can think of Creative Systems Theory's framework for understanding purpose, change, and interrelationship in human systems as a set of tools for making culturally mature, context-specific distinctions. That it succeeds at doing so brings us back to the topic of this book. We can understand the theory's ability to address context in terms of how Integrative Meta-perspective provides a more direct connection with intelligence's multiple aspects. When we draw on the whole of intelligence's creative multiplicity and do so in the needed, more conscious and integrative ways, the fact that truth is contextual becomes obvious.

Here I'll reflect briefly on two kinds of contextual relativity addressed by Creative Systems Theory, giving particular attention to intelligence's role in addressing them. The first, what the theory calls Patterning in Time, deals with the way intelligence's multiplicity manifests in specific ways with each stage in any creative/formative process. The second, Patterning in Space notions, address here-and-now contextual relativity. They make a similarly dynamic and nuanced kind of discernment for systemic differences at specific points in time—for example, between domains in culture, academic disciplines, groups with different ideological leanings, or individuals with differing personality styles. The Creative Systems Personality Typology[14] provides the most developed set of Patterning in Space distinctions in the theory.

Patterning in Time

Patterning in Time concepts highlight how culturally mature decision-making requires being keenly attentive to temporal context. With maturity in our personal development, we get a beginning sense of such relativity as it pertains to our individual lives. We better recognize how different an experience can be depending on when in our lives it takes place. We may also come to better appreciate differences that are a function of where we are developmentally in activities we engage in—in a relationship, in a job, in a particular creative endeavor. Such a temporal perspective is part of what we call wisdom.

With Cultural Maturity, we gain a similar ability to step back and recognize the role of change in how we understand more broadly. That includes an even deeper and more developed appreciation for such more personal-scale, change-related differences. And of particular importance, it also includes more encompassing, cultural-level temporal understanding. Sensitivity to one's

---

[14] See Charles M. Johnston, MD, *The Creative Systems Personality Typology: Engaging the Generative Roots of Diversity*, 2023, ICD Press.

temporal context at a cultural level has always been important, but in times past it came with being immersed in one's cultural time—like water to a fish. Integrative Meta-perspective is needed if we are to understand ourselves consciously and deeply in the context of cultural time. And certainly, it is necessary if we are to appreciate the temporal contexts of others.

As far as that deeper appreciation for personal-scale change-related differences that comes with culturally mature understanding, applying developmental perspective to individual psychological growth is today generally accepted. But it is important to recognize that even that is quite recent. I've noted the influence of Jean Piaget's work early on in my thinking. His ideas were then groundbreaking. Concepts that apply evolutionary perspective to cultural change tend not only to be less recognized, in certain academic circles they can be specifically suspect, if not outright dismissed. This is in part for good reasons. Evolutionary thinking has been used in times past to justify racism and colonialism. But the primary reason is likely deeper. It turns out that it takes Integrative Meta-perspective and its fuller engagement with intelligence's multiplicity to appreciate cultural evolution in any deep way.

In my book, *Intelligence's Creative Multiplicity*[15], I look at how intelligence manifests in different ways with each stage in creative/formative process introduced the connection. With Cultural Maturity's cognitive changes and the capacity to engage our multiple intelligences more directly and more fully, we become better able to recognize the kinds of richness that order the realities of different cultural times. The ability to make sense of cultural change in a way that is deeply affirming of human experience, whatever the period in culture, lets us get beyond past objections to evolutionary perspective. The result is a nuance and complexity of understanding that is essential if we are to effectively

---

[15] Charles M. Johnston, MD, Intelligence's Creative Multiplicity: And Its Critical Role in the Future of Understanding, 2023, ICD Press.

move forward.

My book *Creative Systems Theory*[16] examines how Patterning in Time notions and their foundation in an appreciation for intelligence's creative multiplicity apply to developmental dynamics of all sorts—a simple creative act, personal psychological development, how love relationships change, how organizations change, and the evolution of culture. Below is a chart from the book that summarizes some of these striking parallels (Figure B-1). In it I include the formal terms that the theory uses for the various creative stages—Pre-Axis for creation's "incubation stage,"

CREATIVE STAGES						
Pre-Axis	Early-Axis	Middle-Axis	Late-Axis	Transition	Integrative Stages	
MAJOR PERIODICITIES						
A CREATIVE EVENT						
Incubation	Inspiration	Perspiration	Finishing & Polishing	Presentation	Becoming "Second Nature" (Integration of the newly created form into self and culture)	
A LIFETIME						
Prenatal Period & Infancy	Childhood	Adolescence	Early Adulthood	Midlife Transition	Mature Adulthood (From knowledge to wisdom—integration of self as formed identity with the ground of being)	
A RELATIONSHIP						
Pre-relationship	Falling in Love	Time of Struggle	Established Relationship	Time of Questioning	Mature Intimacy (Relationship as two whole people—marriage of the "loved" and the "lover" within each person)	
THE HISTORY OF CULTURE						
Pre-History	Golden Ages	Middle Ages	Age of Reason	Transitional Culture	Cultural Maturity (Larger meeting of the form and context of culture)	

Fig. B-1: Patterning in Time[17]

---

[16] Charles M. Johnston, MD, Creative Systems Theory: A Comprehensive Theory of Purpose, Change, and Interrelationship in Human Systems (with Particular Pertinence to Understanding the Times We Live In and the Tasks Ahead for the Species), 2021, ICD Press.

[17] You will notice that the chart includes a depiction of how polarity evolves over the course of any creative/formative process. Previously, I've described how the distance between polar opposites increases with each stage in formative process's first half and how formative process's second half involves more specifically integrative dynamics. Creative Systems Theory calls this progression the Creative Function.

Early-Axis for "inspiration stage" dynamics, Middle-Axis for creation's "perspiration stage," and Late-Axis for its "finishing and polishing" stage. You will see the reason for including this more formal language shortly when we turn to Patterning in Space distinctions.

The way Integrative Meta-perspective alters our relationship to history provides one of the best ways to appreciate the power of applying intelligence's creative multiplicity to our understanding of change. Oscar Wilde wrote, "The one duty we owe to history is to rewrite it." By bringing culturally mature evolutionary perspective and intelligence's creative multiplicity to how we address history, Creative Systems Theory's application of a creative frame does just that.

Its contribution in this regard has multiple layers. Most immediately, drawing creatively on the whole of intelligence results in a more dynamic picture of history, one that in new ways comes alive. Traditional notions of history tend to reduce the past to a chronicling of leaders, wars, and technologies. And more recent "big history" efforts rarely get us much further. The picture provided by a creative frame at the least has as much to do with us as what we might invent. And ultimately it has to do with something more fundamental—how collectively we create the structures of human societies and the truths on which we base our lives.

Creative Systems Theory Patterning in Time concepts also help us see history more accurately. Certainly, this is the case where traditionally we have denigrated the realities of earlier cultural times. Patterning in Time observations provide an appreciation for what makes the realities of various chapters in humanity's story powerful and unique, including those we may have painted darkly before. It is here that they most directly address the legitimate concerns that have often in times past resulted in the dismissal of evolutionary thinking.

Just as much, Patterning in Time concepts help us see history more accurately where in the past we have romantically idealized particular cultural realities. Such idealizations have taken different forms depending on the time in culture that was romanticized.[18] But whatever the reference, Integrative Meta-perspective similarly helps us leave behind this more elevating sort of projective distortion. Cultural Maturity's cognitive reordering provides a clearer, if not always so reflexively affirming, picture of the past.

Patterning in Time notions also contribute by making how we understand history deeper and more complete. Even when denigrating and idealizing have not distorted our perceptions, the sensibilities that have defined Modern Age thought have caused us to miss much that is most important. Culturally Mature perspective helps us better recognize how aspects of history to which we may have given secondary importance at best—such as art, music, religion, moral belief, or the life of the body—in fact have considerable pertinence to making sense of the past. And it turns out that what we have missed has often been exactly that which is most essential not to miss if we wish to make sense of values, motivations, and worldviews—particularly those of premodern peoples (including ourselves prior to the Industrial Age). With Cultural Maturity's cognitive reordering, these added ingredients stop being condiments and become explicit parts of the main meal.

As important, Patterning in Time notions provide a picture that makes history as much about "why" as about "what." Culturally mature developmental/evolutionary perspective helps us better put past events in context and grasp how one moment of history ties to another—insights that can radically alter how we interpret circumstances. It transforms history from a chronicling of events and beliefs to a multifaceted study of human purpose

---

18   Romantic idealization can form associations with any cultural stage. Academics may idealize the Age of Reason (or sometimes the ancient Greeks). Adamant conservative and fundamentalist religious views can by inference idealize almost medieval sensibilities (drawing on belief from a time before modern secular humanism and after the rise of monotheism). And New Age ideologies, along with the beliefs of environmentalists and certain feminists, may draw on idealized references to cultural times and places where archetypally feminine sensibilities held clear influence—for example, to tribal cultures, early agrarian societies, and classical Eastern belief.

and our relationship to it. While purpose has always been a part of well-told history, when we consciously bring more of ourselves to the task of understanding, history becomes more specifically an inquiry into who we are as storytellers and makers of meaning. Also, by implication, history becomes as much about the possible nature of meaning in the future as it is about the stories that have brought us to where we are today.

Finally, Creative Systems Theory Patterning in Time notions suggest an important "historical" reward beyond history itself. They make the study of history a hands-on tool for acquiring culturally mature perspective. Just as practicing needed new leadership capacities or more deeply engaging the complexities of intelligence can bring us closer to culturally mature understanding, so too can a sufficiently deep engagement with where we have come from. Grasping history more deeply can provide a particularly powerful way to realize the more complete kind of understanding that future tasks of all sorts will increasingly require of us.

Patterning in Space

Creative Systems Theory's approach to understanding contextual relativity is unusual in that it addresses both temporal distinctions and here-and-now differences. It is unique as far as I know in conceptually linking these two kinds of contextual relativity. In times past, if we've acknowledged contextual differences at all, we've assumed that these two kinds of differences were distinct concerns. I've noted how Creative Systems Theory uses the same creative language when making Patterning in Time and Patterning in Space distinctions. With Integrative Meta-perspective—and specifically with the application of a creative frame—we find that a related kind of mapping helps us understand both change and interrelationship in human systems.

Creative Systems Theory describes how human systems pattern creatively not just over time, but also in the here and now. Biological systems inhabit ecological niches. Creative Systems Theory proposes that human systems similarly differentiate into a predictable array of creatively ordered psychological/social niches. Patterning in Space concepts address diversity within human systems of all scales—domains in a society, departments in a university, professions, functions in a business, roles in a family, personality styles, or parts within ourselves. Over the years, Patterning in Space distinctions have provided many of Creative Systems Theory's most fascinating insights. They've also offered some of the most rewarding—and fun—interactions with colleagues and students.

While Creative Systems Patterning in Space concepts are pertinent any time our interest lies with human here-and-now systemic differences, it is with personality style differences that this aspect of the theory had its beginnings and also where it has been most developed. The Creative Systems Personality Typology (CSPT) presents a nuanced and detailed framework for teasing apart and articulating temperament differences.

It is remarkable how different people can be as a product of temperament. Just as remarkable is how blind we can be to this fact. If we take time to understand personality diversity at all deeply, it can be hard to imagine that teachers could teach effectively without such understanding or that psychologists could in any way be of help. And we find such blindness with the most learned of people. As with Patterning in Time's evolutionary notions, attempts within academia to delineate and articulate personality differences tend not to be widely acknowledged and are often simply dismissed.[19]

It is reasonable to ask how it is that we have tended to miss this profundity of difference. I suspect the reason is related. Again, we find a kind of distinction

---

[19] The one exception is the Myers-Briggs typology (based on the work of Carl Jung) that is often used by people in psychology and business consulting. But the CSPT engages differences with significantly greater depth and with implications that more directly address the tasks of Cultural Maturity.

where understanding requires that we draw on the whole of intelligence's multiplicity. We need to get at least a toe in Cultural Maturity's new territory of experience if this kind of difference is to make deep sense.

In Chapter Six, I briefly discussed how temperament and personality style can influence a person's approach to Parts Work. The Creative Systems Personality Typology provides a way to understand not just the specific strengths and weaknesses of different personality styles, but also how various styles can best work together. It also offers a framework for understanding how personality diversity interplays with other kinds of human differences, such as gender and ethnic diversity. And it provides perspective for making sense of the experiences of people with different temperaments at specific points in developmental processes. It has particular significance for its power as a tool for supporting the kind of creative collaboration on which a healthy future will depend more and more.

A bare-boned look at how Creative Systems Theory approaches temperament differences begins with the recognition that people with different personality styles are most gifted regarding the various sensibilities that I've associated with specific stages in formative process. (They most embody the intelligences and relationships between polar tendencies needed to support stage-specific creative tasks.) Using Creative Systems Theory language, more "Early-Axis" types have greatest natural affinity with more "inspiration stage" sensibilities, more "Middle-Axis" types with more "perspiration stage" sensibilities, and more "Late-Axis" types with more "finishing and polishing" sensibilities.

We can identify the basic contours of Early-, Middle-, and Late-Axis personality differences readily in the goings-on of daily life. (As I will get back to, Pre-Axial personality dynamics represent a special case in modern culture.) For example, within a business, we have the wild creatives and nerdy "eggheads" over in research and development. We also have the managers and workers who take R and D's innovations and get them first into a practical form and then into production. And we have the marketing and financial types who add ideas about what is needed to make the product attractive to its buyers, take care of money matters, and do the selling.

The fact of Early-, Middle-, and Late-Axis difference is only the starting point when applying the typology. Within each personality style axis, the theory also distinguishes more Upper and Lower, Outer and Inner "aspects" and personality constellations. We know these differences from everyday experience. Some people live mostly from their heads or from similarly elevated spiritual aspects of experience, while others are more down to earth. Some people give greatest attention to more in-the-world concerns, while with others more personal, internal elements in experience have the greater importance.

On the CSPT website (**www.CSPThome.org**) and in the book *Creative Systems Theory*, I go into detail regarding each of the theory's basic temperament patterns. Here I will touch only on the basic contours of the typology, giving particular attention to the role of intelligence's multiplicity. In describing each personality style axis, I will note how it preferentially engages and applies specific aspects of our cognitive complexity. Later I will come back and fill out these basic intelligence-related observations as I did with Patterning in Time. In a similar way, with each personality style pattern, along with one intelligence having primary influence, we can find each of the other intelligences present, but in a secondary way specific to that temperament axis.

Pre-Axial Patterns

Pre-Axial patterns differ from other temperament constellations in that they rarely manifest in modern times as primary dynamics in healthy individuals (the one exception being people with a strongly Pre-Axial cultural background). Because such dynamics are principally of interest to those in the helping professions, they are beyond the scope of this discussion of normal variation.

I will observe simply that body intelligence tends to play a major role in how they process experience.

Early-Axis Patterns

Early-Axis temperaments reflect a special affinity with the inspiration stage in formative process—that period when the buds of new creation first find their way into the world of the manifest. The Early's defining intelligence is the imaginal, the language of symbol, myth, and metaphor (for the modern Early, as experienced within the rational/material context of today's Late-Axis culture), with body intelligence playing a secondary role. The reality of the Early-Axis individual is born from the organizing sensibilities that give us possibility and innovation.

A few notable Earlies from history: Leonardo da Vinci, Georgia O'Keeffe, Rainer Maria Rilke, Isadora Duncan, Mary Cassatt, Howard Hughes, John Coltrane, Boris Karloff, Pablo Picasso, Frank Zappa, Nikola Tesla, Jack Nicholson, and Mrs. Saunders (my kindergarten teacher). More notorious Earlies include Charles Manson, David Kaczynski, and Rasputin.

The pivotal role of imaginal intelligence is most explicit with Early/Uppers. I am reminded of Albert Einstein's famous assertion, "I am interested in God's thoughts; the rest are details." Or from Lewis Carroll in Through the Looking Glass: "'Contrariwise,' continued Tweedledee, 'if it was so, it might be; and if it were so, it would be: but as it isn't, it ain't. That is logic.'" With Early/Lowers, body intelligence can play at least as great a role. Early/Lowers tend to be more comfortable in their bodies than other temperaments and derive particular fulfillment through bodily experience. Indeed, for Early/Lowers body and spirit can be hard to distinguish. Salvador Dali once exclaimed, "I don't do drugs—I am drugs."

Where do we find Earlies? Often, they work with young children (a grade school teacher, a day-care worker). Frequently they become artists—visual artists (particularly those of more abstract inclination), dancers (particularly those whose aesthetic tends toward the improvisational), musicians (most jazz musicians, some classical and many rock and roll musicians), or writers (particularly poets and most writers of science fiction). Earlies also make important contributions in the sciences. (Many of science's major innovators have been Earlies—though the larger number of scientists are Lates.) Recently, Earlies have starred in the high-tech revolution. (Steve Jobs, Bill Gates, and Elon Musk are all Earlies.) Most people who teach reflective techniques such as meditation and yoga are Earlies. (It is the Earlies who are most attracted to things spiritual, particularly practices with roots in Early-Axis cultural times.)

Middle-Axis Patterns

Middle-Axis temperaments most strongly embody the "perspiration" stage sensibilities that we find as new creation struggles into crude, but now solid, manifestation. While Earlies identify most with the first improvisational sparks of creation, Middles find greatest meaning turning sparks into usable fire. Emotional-moral intelligence, the intelligence of heart and guts (as it manifests within Late-Axis culture) orders the Middle's world.

A few notable Middles from history: Teddy Roosevelt, Mother Teresa, Margaret Thatcher, Joe Louis, Billy Graham, Babe Ruth, Florence Nightingale, Colin Powell, Aretha Franklin, Julia Child, Queen Victoria, Johnny Cash, J. Edgar Hoover, Cesar Chavez, and Betty Friedan. More notorious Middles include Joseph Stalin, Adolf Hitler, Ma Barker, and Jesse James.

The harder aspects of emotional-moral intelligence—the stuff of guts and fortitude—dominate with Middle/Upper and Middle/Outer temperaments. From Winston Churchill, "This is a lesson: Never give in—never, never, never, never." From Samuel Johnson, "Great works are performed not by strength, but by perseverance." The stuff of the heart holds sway in Middle/Inner and Middle/Lower temperaments, where the archetypally feminine is strongest.

From Margaret Mead, "One of the oldest human needs is having someone wonder where you are when you don't come home at night." From Abraham Lincoln, "The better part of a man's life consists of his friendships."

Middles often become teachers, managers in business, social workers, soldiers, athletes and coaches, union bosses, ministers or priests, physicians (about an equal balance of Middle/Upper and Late/Upper), politicians (a similar balance), police officers, fire fighters, bankers, loggers, owners of family businesses, machinists, miners, or carpenters. In addition, the Middles make up the greater portion of stay-at-home parents. (It is with Middle-Axis that we find the strongest identification with home, family, and community.) Women who think of themselves first as wives and mothers are commonly Middles, as are the most devoted husbands and fathers. Middle-Axis individuals frequently play strong roles in their neighborhoods and churches, and in social service organizations. Most of the "real work" in society is done by Middles.

Late-Axis Patterns

Late-Axis patterns correspond to the finishing and polishing stage in formative process. People with Late-Axis temperaments draw on sensibilities that make them particularly gifted when it comes to tasks of detail and completion. Here rational/material intelligence orders experience, bringing emphasis to the intellect and to the more refined (manifest) aspects of the emotional and the aesthetic.

Some notable Lates from history: Walter Cronkite, Marie Curie, Carl Sagan, Julia Roberts, Sammy Davis, Jr., Elizabeth Taylor, Frank Sinatra, Gloria Steinem, Woodrow Wilson, Johnny Carson, Clark Gable, Mikhail Baryshnikov, William F. Buckley, and Robert Redford. Less savory sorts tend to engage in white collar crime, so are less visible and less often prosecuted than Early and Late lawbreakers—Michael Milken comes to mind, along with those involved in the investment bank excesses of the 2008 financial collapse.

The aspects of rational/material intelligence that most stand out with people of Late/Upper temperament are clarity of thought, verbal facility, and the ability to deal easily and effectively with the material world. From John F. Kennedy, "In times of turbulence and change, it is more true than ever that knowledge is power." From Elizabeth Cady Stanton, "In a word, I am always busy, which is perhaps the chief reason I am always well." With Late/Lower personalities, the aesthetic combines with more material aspects of emotional intelligence. From Alfred Lord Tennyson, "'Tis better to have loved and lost, than never to have loved at all." Estée Lauder offered this advice: "Never just 'run out for a few minutes' without looking your best. This is not vanity—it is self-liking."

Lates often become professors, writers, lawyers, CEOs, scientists, fashion models, ballet or modern dancers, Wall Street financiers, marketers, or actors. More frequently than with people from other axes, various individuals can differ widely in their inclinations.[20] Within Late-Axis we find the people who are most rational in their perspective, and also those who tend most toward the romantic. We find the people who are most materialistically driven, and at once many of those most committed to artistic and intellectual pursuits where monetary remuneration can be slight. We find the people most aggressively in the world, and also many of those most internal and reflective in their proclivities.

With Late/Upper/Inners, the more intellectual of these qualities stand out. University professors, scientific researchers, and nonfiction writers commonly have Late/Upper/Inner personalities. With Late/Upper/Outers, more external and material concerns take center stage. Here we commonly find the people who are most facile with money and the complexities of the business world—corporate executives, economists, media moguls, and stockbrokers.

---

[20] A look to the Creative Function provides explanation. It is here that we see the greatest natural separation between poles.

With Late/Lower patterns, qualities such as social ease, talent, sensuality, and emotional presence often most stand out. Of all personality groups, Late/Lowers are most likely to enjoy being "on stage." People in the performing arts tend to have at least some Late/Lower in their makeup, as do the great majority of fashion models and television entertainers. Late/Lower/Inner is a common personality style of dancers and actors. With Late/Lower/Outers we find the people with the greatest capacity to project and be visible. They define the entertainment industry. Glamour and celebrity are Late/Lower/Outer words.

More than one temperament, one intelligence

I've noted an important Patterning in Space, intelligence-related recognition that we also encounter with Patterning in Time. While one intelligence has primary influence with each personality style pattern, we also find each of the other intelligences present in a secondary way specific to that temperament axis. Appreciating how this is so helps fill out our understanding of each temperament constellation. It also further deepens our understanding of each of intelligence's multiple aspects by highlighting the diverse ways in which it can manifest. And there is a further implication. The fact that we find such nuance in parallels between Patterning in Time and Patterning in Space distinction provides further confirmation of the power of a creative frame and the kind of cognitive reordering that Creative Systems Theory describes with the concept of Integrative Meta-perspective.

Below I've drawn on language from *Intelligence's Creative Multiplicity* (Figure 3-1) with a few reflections that help tie observations to temperament distinctions. The important recognition is that with very little adjustment, the same words apply equally well to making temporal and here-and-now contextual observations. (Again, I should note that finding good words for these more detailed distinctions necessarily presents a challenge, particularly where intelligences don't function at the level of language.)

Body Intelligence: I've observed that body intelligence is primary with Pre-Axis. The way I describe it in the chart— "the creature body/the body as nature"—works pretty well. In the chart, I describe the Early-Axis body as "the body as essence/the body of ritual/the spirit or dream body." A term like "energetic body" works better when thinking about personality dynamics. It is how we experience the body when doing yoga or meditating. The way the chart describes the Middle-Axis body— "the visceral-muscular body/the body of heart and guts"—again works adequately. It is the bodily reality that we most associate with being an athlete and that we feel most directly in relationships. In the chart, I describe the Late-Axis body as "the physical body/the body as appearance." This is the body as experienced when we say we "have" a body (as if it was separate from us). It is also the body that Sophia Loren was referring to when she observed that "sex appeal is fifty percent what you've got and fifty percent what people think you've got."

Imaginal Intelligence: While the symbolic has its strongest influence with Early-Axis temperaments, it similarly plays a role and takes manifestations with each axis. In the chart, I describe its role with Pre-Axis as "animism—the symbolic as a language of nature." This fits as well for temperament as it does for creative stage. For Early-Axis, the chart describes imaginal intelligence's manifestation as "myth—the symbolic as a language of ritual and inspirational relationship." With Early-Axis temperaments, it works better to think of it in terms of creative imagination. The chart describes Middle-Axis imaginal expression as "legend—the symbolic as a language of moral order." With Middle-Axis personality styles, we might think of the symbolism a person associates with their religious or national affiliations. In the chart, I describe imaginal intelligence as it manifests in Late-Axis as "fantasy—the symbolic as a language of romanticism and idealism." The word "fantasy" works well for temperament as well as development. Here we find the more surface kind of imagination found on a visit to Disneyland.

Emotional Intelligence: I've observed that emotional intelligence's influence is primary with Middle-Axis temperaments. Its role is less explicit with Pre-Axis, but the chart's description of "feeling as harmony with nature" certainly implies emotional sensibility. The kind of body intelligence that is primary at this stage can be deeply felt. The chart describes emotional intelligence in Early-Axis with the words "feeling as inspiration, essence, and primal passion." That works well for emotional intelligence's manifestation with Early-Axis temperament. How the chart describes emotional intelligence with Middle-Axis— "feeling as visceral emotion"—works adequately all the way around. I've described emotional intelligence as the intelligence of "heart and guts." That kind of language is most in keeping with its Middle-Axis manifestations. The chart describes the feeling dimension with Late-Axis as "feeling as sentiment and pleasure." That continues to work well for temperament, particularly as it manifests with Late/Lower patterns.

Rational Intelligence: While the intellect takes most developed manifestation with Late-Axis in both time and space, every temperament axis has its own version of verbal/ideational expression rooted in its underlying sensibilities. In the chart, I refer to its presence with Pre-Axis as "participatory consciousness." While body intelligence is primary with Pre-Axial dynamics, there is at least self-concept and, with it, ideas about the connectedness of experience. With Early-Axis in the chart, I refer to "magical and aesthetic thought". Early/Uppers often think in highly sophisticated ways, but their ideas ultimately serve creative insight. With Middle-Axis, the chart refers to "the logic of right and wrong." That works well for Patterning in Space as well as

Patterning in Time. The ideas of Middles tend to refer in some way to issues of morality, competence, relationship, or control. The chart speaks of rational intelligence with Late-Axis as "Rational, material thought." Regarding temperament, here we find rational logic of the academic sort. We also find acumen when it comes to finance. And particularly with Late/Lower, we find the kind of aesthetic distinctions that allow one to be adept at performance.

INDEX

A

Assagioli, Roberto 17, 73

B

Big-Picture Questions, 7, 58
bodily intelligence, 103
Bridging, 95

C

Capacitance, 20, 105
cognitive complexity, 7, 8, 88, 123
cognitive reordering, 8, 73, 86, 88, 90, 92, 94, 95, 100, 105, 108, 114, 119, 128
cognitive rewiring, 15
comfort with uncertainty and complexity, 8, 109
Compromise Fallacies, 21
conflict, 10, 31, 37, 38, 39, 43, 49, 65, 77, 103, 109
Creative Nature of Truth, 77
Creative Systems Personality Typology, 4, 79, 80, 87, 91, 105, 115, 121, 122
Creative Systems Theory, 4, 7, 8, 9, 10, 14, 19, 20, 21, 33, 38, 72, 77, 78, 79, 81, 84, 85, 86, 87, 88, 89, 90, 91, 92, 93, 94, 95, 96, 97, 100, 101, 104, 105, 106, 108, 112, 113, 114, 115, 117, 118, 120, 122, 123, 128
Crisis of Purpose, 4, 32, 33, 70, 100
Cultural Maturity, 4, 7, 8, 9, 10, 16, 37, 48, 56, 64, 73, 84, 85, 86, 87, 88, 89, 90, 92, 93, 94, 95, 99, 103, 104, 106, 107, 108, 109, 110, 112, 113, 114, 115, 116, 119, 121, 122
culturally mature capacity, 19
culturally mature leadership, 11, 12, 15, 19, 22, 86
culturally mature perspective, 9, 11, 14, 21, 37, 57, 75, 80, 87, 94, 99, 120
culturally mature understanding, 15, 18, 19, 21, 73, 81, 86, 87, 98, 99, 100, 116, 120
culture as a creative process, 8

D

Dilemma of Trajectory, 106, 107, 108, 111, 112

E

Early-, Middle-, and Late-Axis difference, 123
Early-Axis Patterns, 124
emotional and moral intelligence, 103
engagement with parts, 18
engaging experience in more conscious and complete ways, 17
extreme polarization, 40

F

Fitzgerald, F. Scott 94, 95
fact of real limits, 8
Fundamental Organizing Concept, 78, 86, 97

G

gender, 20, 58, 64, 65, 67, 82, 122
Gestalt therapy, 17, 73

H

History of Belief, 81

I

identity, 6, 10, 16, 17, 23, 46, 48, 51, 66, 72, 74, 76, 82, 87, 93, 99, 103, 109, 110
imaginal intelligence, 103, 124, 129

Institute for Creative Development, 4, 5, 6, 85
Integrative Meta-perspective, 9, 11, 12, 15, 17, 23, 40, 71, 73, 76, 81, 88, 89, 90, 91, 92, 93, 94, 98, 100, 107, 110, 112, 114, 116, 118, 119, 120, 128
integrity, 67, 93, 109
intelligence's multiple aspects, 17, 18, 98, 114, 128
intelligence's multiplicity, 78, 92, 95, 98, 100, 106, 115, 116, 122, 123

L

Late-Axis Patterns, 126
leadership statements, 18, 24

M

Major Life Choices, 28
mechanistic thinking, 85
Middle-Axis Patterns, 125
Moreno, Jacob 17, 73
Multiple Intelligences, 77

N

Nature of the Self, 76

P

Parenting, 52
Parts Work, 7, 8, 9, 10, 11, 12, 13, 15, 16, 17, 18, 19, 20, 21, 22, 23, 24, 30, 33, 37, 38, 40, 43, 44, 45, 47, 48, 49, 50, 51, 52, 54, 58, 59, 61, 62, 65, 67, 68, 70, 71, 72, 73, 74, 75, 76, 77, 78, 79, 80, 81, 82, 122
Patterning in Space, 86, 105, 115, 118, 120, 121, 128, 130
Patterning in Time, 86, 101, 104, 115, 117, 118, 119, 120, 121, 123, 128, 131
Perl, Fritz 17, 73
personality constellations, 79, 123
Piaget, Jean 116
polar fallacies, 21, 78
polarities, 21, 81, 92, 100
polarized relationships, 18

Pre-Axial patterns, 123
psychodrama, 17, 73
psychodynamics, 74, 76, 82
Psychopathology, 80
psychosynthesis, 17, 73

Q

questions of purpose, 67, 70

R

rational intelligence, 102, 103, 131
relationships, 8, 10, 20, 22, 30, 39, 48, 49, 50, 51, 65, 66, 71, 72, 76, 77, 81, 85, 86, 89, 90, 91, 92, 93, 96, 99, 100, 101, 105, 107, 110, 111, 117, 122, 129

S

Separative Fallacies, 21
social/political dynamics, 74
Symptoms, 20, 105
systemically holding experience as a whole, 16

T

technological advancement, 58, 59
Temperament, 6, 79
training of therapists, 75
Transitional Absurdity, 4, 106, 108, 112

U

Unity Fallacies, 21, 61
Upper and Lower, Outer and Inner "aspects, 123

W

whole-box-of-crayons complexity, 11
Whole-Person chair, 11, 12, 17, 18, 20, 23, 27, 29, 30, 33, 34, 40, 50, 51, 52, 53, 54, 55, 56, 57, 59, 66, 71, 72, 74, 75
Whole-System perspective chair, 12, 22

www.ingramcontent.com/pod-product-compliance
Lightning Source LLC
LaVergne TN
LVHW020438070526
838199LV00063B/4777